Something
Beyond Nothing?

Something Beyond Nothing?

The God We Don't Yet Know

Brian Niece

Foreword by Dan Boone

WIPF & STOCK · Eugene, Oregon

SOMETHING BEYOND NOTHING?
The God We Don't Yet Know

Wipf & Stock
An Imprint of Wipf and Stock Publishers
199 W. 8th Ave., Suite 3
Eugene, OR 97401

www.wipfandstock.com

PAPERBACK ISBN: 978-1-5326-3586-1
HARDCOVER ISBN: 978-1-5326-3588-5
EBOOK ISBN: 978-1-5326-3587-8

Manufactured in the U.S.A.   JUNE 27, 2018

For all who live in the questions

Contents

Foreword

To Life

THE UNEXAMINED LIFE IS not worth living. Really? Most of the people I know are living exactly that life. They rise, they eat, they work, they sleep. Like the sun making its circle around the earth (ancient cosmology here), they rise to repeat the same cycle until the breath given them at birth returns to the one who gave it. Then we gather for their funeral and contemplate in eulogy the meaning of their life.

Into this routine comes Ecclesiastes—this philosophical, questioning, somewhat sarcastic, snarly book of pointed jabs at the unquestioning life most of us have determined we will live. It is an awkward book, so awkward that most of us who wrestle with it are quite sure that some later editor penned an epilogue in Ecclesiastes 12 to try to make sense of the rambling vanity we have just read. But like most eulogies, they never quite get at the meaning that was pursued in the day-to-day routine.

You are about to read another odd book. If you like how-to books, answer books, "ah-ha I have discovered it" books, you may get lost in this one. By page thirty you will be saying, "Where is he going?" By page sixty you will be saying, "OK, I'm a little intrigued." By page ninety, you may conclude, "This is an honest assessment of life as I am experiencing it when I dare to let my bald questions come out of the closet."

Ecclesiastes is for the person who dares examine routine life and the unpredictability behind it. It is for the one who appreciates wisdom as a guide, but knows that the pithy proverbs are more like probabilities than promises of how things will turn out when we live a certain way. It is about being human, humus, dependent dust, earthy beings who expire. It is about accepting these things about ourselves without some angry, anxious attempt to prove it all wrong by elevating ourselves to divine status. It is about Christian humanism. And in the end, it is about receiving work and play and food and drink as gift, not clutching it too tightly as if it is the trinket that justifies our existence. And then, it is finally about letting it go . . . back to the God who gave it, with a worshipful heart of gratitude that we have been graced beyond our doing by the act of being human.

I commend the work of my friend to you and trust that you will suspend the kind of judgement that gets to the point so you can check the box and get on to the next thing that proves your life is worthwhile. Just stop. Examine your life in view of the gift of Ecclesiastes and the words of this book. If the end of these pages finds you more humble, less frittering, and deeply worshipful, you will have received the gift that was intended.

Dan Boone

Preface

SINCE I'VE HAD TWO previous careers—one in professional theatre and one in the church—this book could not help but be influenced by many things that have tutored me, walked with me, suffered by me, and shaped my modes of communication. So in what follows you will find non–fiction and fiction. You will find scriptural interpretation and poetic meditation. You will find theological reflection and a script for a short scene. You will find material and phrases which might make you think, "That's really something." You will find other chapters and sentences which might make you think, "That's a whole bunch of nothing." I've been an actor, a director, a scriptwriter, a theatrical designer, a pastor, a preacher, a teacher, and a speaker. Elements of all these things are sprinkled in these pages.

"Why not pick one thing and stick to it?" someone might ask. To this I humbly and honestly reply that I am incapable of such a feat. To single out one thing is to lessen my whole. This amalgam of trajectories makes me who I am. And who I am influences how I read the world, how I communicate what I see, and how I question both the world and myself.

This book was born out of my years-long fascination with that strange book entitled Ecclesiastes. Is it my favorite book in the scriptural canon? No. But it's one that continually makes me uncomfortable. This book is some of the fleshing out of this discomfort. And I hope there is some small thing in this work that will make you just a bit uncomfortable, too.

This book is not wholly academic, nor is it wholly intended for mass public appeal. It is not only for the Christian segment of North American society, nor is it only for those not affiliated with religion. I have attempted to minimize the number of footnotes to a ridiculously small amount for the ease of reading. The bibliography holds what I reference, but it is not exhaustive of the works that influenced this book. I imagine there are parts of this book that will find a home in the academy, parts that will find a home in the church, parts that will find a home in skeptic circles, and parts that will find a home in individual minds and hearts. In that sense, I don't envy my publishers in the marketing of this book.

I wish to thank a few folks who made this possible. I'm grateful to peers, colleagues, friends, and mentors who provided feedback on various parts of the book. You know who you are, and you will likely see your influence in places. I cannot adequately express my gratefulness to my family. My wife, Heather, displays such grace in sharing life with me, not to mention when I'm trying to write a book. Our three children provided not only material for the book, but support and understanding when hearing, "Dad has to go write." My parents helped so much with initial proofing of content and grammar, and making sure I was saying what I was trying to say. My in-laws graciously kept the kids when my wife and I just needed a few hours to ourselves. I'm also amazed that Wipf & Stock Publishers took a chance on this quirky book. To all of the above, thank you.

How to Read This Book

MOST BOOKS ARE INTENDED to be read from the first page to the last page in direct succession. This book certainly has an arc that bends in that direction. But each of the chapters can also stand alone. So, you are free to finish the Prelude and go directly to chapter 1. But you may, at this very moment, be interested in hearing what an argument between Friedrich Nietzsche and G. K. Chesterton would be like. In that case, you should head for chapter 4, where you can be a fly on the pub wall where these two fascinating historical minds meet. Also, right now you may be wondering, "Just what does a fictionalized conversation between Nietzsche and Chesterton have to do with Ecclesiastes?" And that is, of course, a valid question. I would answer that Ecclesiastes is our primary lens, or our major guide for exploring something beyond nothing, yet Nietzsche and Chesterton have something to say about one of the persistent questions that the writer of Ecclesiastes raises. And if we let them have their say, we may catch a glimpse into something about the God that we don't yet know. Also . . . at some point you may be feeling a bit bewildered by the non-linear approach of this book. In that case, I would recommend one of the interludes sprinkled among the chapters, wherein God is reimagined through the eyes of wonder and poetry. There you can reflect and catch your breath.

What I'm getting at is that you can read this book in any manner and any order you wish, and your choice will be right. Maybe I read one too many Choose-Your-Own-Adventure books as a child.

But there is something paradoxically freeing about being granted a modicum of control. In fact, the writer of Ecclesiastes keenly perceives the illusion of freedom through control that the journey of life can bring. So, immerse yourself in the illusion, just for a while. Pick a place in this book to go next. Or just read straight through. It's your choice. And one more thing: if you are thinking that such an approach is rather useless, I'd point you to chapter 1, where we might discover that there is usefulness to uselessness.

Prelude

The Elephant in the Room, or How Did Ecclesiastes Get Included in Scripture?

When there's an elephant in the room, introduce him.

—RANDY PAUSCH

WHAT YOU ARE ABOUT to read is at times storytelling, a theological analysis, scriptural exegesis, dialogue between transhistorical thinkers, glimpses of philosophy, and meditational interludes, among other things. At its core, this book is an experiment in finding—perhaps making—meaning. And it is the journey of the finding, not necessarily the thing which is found, that takes precedence. Though the biblical book of Ecclesiastes will be our lens for viewing this experiment, along the way we will be influenced by existential philosophers, Christian humanist thinkers, theologians of various persuasions, drama, storytelling, and whatever else seems relevant to the journey. My hope is that you will be surprised on occasion, just like I was surprised in the process. You might also be challenged to think differently, to wrestle with difficult questions, and to not be satisfied with easy answers, just like I continue to be when I meditate on this material.

Oh, and something else: I haven't written this book as an expert dispensing wisdom to those who may one day make it to my level. I'm not the wizard Gandalf, with several lifetimes of experience and education at my beck and call, handing out prescient knowledge piecemeal for you to discover. Sticking with the Tolkien metaphor, you might think of me more as Strider, aka Aragorn, who has been up the path a little way, taken some wrong turns, learned just as much through suffering and failure as through success (maybe more so). Yes, I'm more the weathered experimenter of this little Fellowship. And if these analogies are lost on you just now, I'd suggest you put this book down immediately and hop to reading *The Lord of the Rings* trilogy first. There you will find something fine and rare. Plus, I can't guarantee this book will not contain additional allusions to that trilogy. I suppose, if you must, it would be okay to take the shortcut and watch the movies. Just be sure you view the director's cuts. I'll wait.

Now, that you're back, what better way for us to begin this prelude than with a viral YouTube video reference?

On September 18, 2007, about a month after receiving the news that he had advanced pancreatic cancer which gave him roughly three to six months of quality life to live, professor Randy Pausch of Carnegie Mellon University gave a raw and inspiring lecture entitled "Achieving Your Childhood Dreams." The recording of this lecture became popular on YouTube and led to a New York Times bestselling book entitled *The Last Lecture*. Knowing his audience was fully aware of his now public diagnosis—Pausch would die ten months later—he began his lecture by noting how his father had told him, "When there's an elephant in the room, introduce him."

This is sage advice. In friendships, we find that relationships are stronger when we admit our vulnerability, trusting that the other will not take advantage of us. This doesn't seem to translate well to larger contexts. Yet, I can't help but wonder if the academy, the church, the corporate landscape, and the political institutions of the western world would do well to name their elephants more often. Why do we so often carry on as if there are no elephants crowding the small rooms of our discourse? Do we find it easier to somehow ignore the very thing we should be talking about? Why do we too often forget or reject the simple wisdom of our ancestors, opting to remain in a perpetual state of intellectual or emotional adolescence?

Enter stage right: the strange book of Ecclesiastes in the Hebrew Scripture. This is the elephant in the room of both the Jewish and Christian forms of Scripture. Likely there are several elephants hiding in plain sight in Scripture, depending on which theological lens, religious tradition, or philosophical slant you choose to look through. The book of Job, what with its promise of theodicy which never seems to answer those lingering questions of evil, seems a curious text. The "letter" to the Hebrews, which reads more like an oratorical performance piece than a letter, stands out. But for the purpose of this book, Ecclesiastes will be the centerpiece of our focus. That Ecclesiastes would be part of the Tanakh—that is, the Hebrew Scripture, or in a different order, the Christian Old Testament—is telling. Here is a text that seems to question much of the wisdom tradition that is sacrosanct in Deuteronomistic thought. This is a school of thought originating in the book of Deuteronomy, which heavily influenced the texts of Joshua, Judges, 1 and 2 Samuel, 1 and 2 Kings, and some of the major prophets among others. In Deuteronomy we read the following:

> If you heed these ordinances, by diligently observing them, the Lord your God will maintain with you the covenant loyalty that he swore to your ancestors; he will love you, bless you, and multiply you; he will bless the fruit of your womb and the fruit of your ground, your grain and your wine and your oil, the increase of your cattle and the issue of your flock, in the land that he swore to your ancestors to give you. You shall be the most blessed of peoples, with neither sterility nor barrenness among you or your livestock. The Lord will turn away from you every illness; all the dread diseases of Egypt that you experienced, he will not inflict on you, but he will lay them on all who hate you. (Deut 7:12–15)

Ecclesiastes does not see such synchronic theology. That is to say, Ecclesiastes questions some core thinking in major Hebrew scriptural texts that don't jive with the understanding of covenantal relationship played out in the life of the community:

> There is a vanity that takes place on earth, that there are righteous people who are treated according to the conduct of the wicked, and there are wicked people who are treated according to the conduct of the righteous. I said that this also is vanity. (Eccl 8:14)

The writer of Ecclesiastes seems to be saying, "Where is the blessing of abundance for the righteous? Where is the curse of sterility for the wicked? I don't see blessings and curses fitting neatly into my reality!" This is just a small example of the conundrums we will get into with this book. For now, I'll simply state that the book of Ecclesiastes is not safe reading if we wish to have a narrative that merely affirms all we think we know.

Any general survey of Scripture would inform the reader that here is a collection of texts that are in dialogue with each other, but do not agree on some seemingly basic premises, and do not get along so easily together. And of all the disagreeable texts in the Bible, Ecclesiastes sure looks like it outdoes everything else in sheer audacity. Here are just some of the reasons Ecclesiastes may be disagreeable:

- The text raises over forty questions, which never seem to be answered directly. Are they rhetorical questions or legitimate queries about meaning?

- God does not play a direct part in the narrative; God's existence seems to be acknowledged but not necessarily helpful to anything in real life;

- There seems to be little hope involved, except in eating and drinking—after which we die;

- The text questions the wisdom tradition exemplified in the histories of Israel and Judah and in the book of Proverbs.

So how did such an audacious text survive the editing process of Jewish thought and get included in the wisdom literature of the Tanakh? And how did it make it into every authorized version of the Christian Bible from Eastern Orthodox to Catholic? Beyond that, how in the world did Ecclesiastes not end up on the cutting room floor during the years of contention that finally yielded the Protestant Bible? I mean, those guys were ruthless! Eastern and Catholic traditions allowed books like Tobit and Judith into their canons. But the Protestants? They said, "No thanks." If any deciding group were to nix the book of Ecclesiastes from sacred text, surely it would be these guys. But pick up any good or bad translation of the Christian Bible today—and, by the way, there's quite a few bad translations around, but that's another story—and you'll find Ecclesiastes in its usual spot between Proverbs and Song of Solomon. Even its placement seems to lend it legitimacy, wedged as it is between a whole book about wisdom and a book named after the dude considered the wisest king in the history of Israel. Maybe its inclusion in the Jewish and Christian canons has to do with the meaning that seems to be gradually breaking through the words of the writer, or speaker, of this text. Maybe it does not have so much to do with the contents somehow cohering with other books of the Bible, but with the contents working to question and refine assumed traditional understandings of things like wisdom, the purpose of work, incarnation, grace, the meaning of life, and finally God. The Jewish faith, after all, takes as its namesake "Israel," which was the name God gave Jacob because of Jacob's penchant for wrestling. You can't very well have a wrestling match if you don't have some opposing forces involved. Our best Christian theologians have always directed us to never read Scripture in isolation, but to keep in our minds the whole tenor of Scripture as we read any one passage. Perhaps diversity and difference are an intended, though too-often-forgotten, part of our spiritual heritage.

Ecclesiastes is clearly here to stay as part of sacred text. Yes, this elephant is in the room, and it is not a docile elephant skittering to the corner of theological interpretation so as to stay out of the way of better known and, perhaps, better understood books of the Bible.

This is an elephant raging with questions, ready to knock over the pillars of our painstakingly constructed worldview.

The most widely known phrase from Ecclesiastes is "vanity of vanities; all is vanity." Among several other things, which we will get into in the following chapters, this phrase means, "Useless, it is all useless." The text is essentially a pontification on the uselessness of life, work, and leisure. At least, this has long been the major traditional understanding of the worldview espoused in Ecclesiastes. To justify its inclusion in the Bible, many thinkers have focused on this uselessness and proceeded to display a fine mental gymnastics routine. For example, there seems to be no direct divine revelation in Ecclesiastes. Ah, so it must be divine revelation precisely because it is devoid of divine revelation! Though there is some hermeneutical merit to this approach, it stops short. Acknowledging the nothing of Ecclesiastes is not enough. Nothing is where we begin in this quirky book. I think that, if we push a little further, we will find something beyond nothing.

We must, however, acknowledge that a speaker who talks all about uselessness and nothingness has some explaining to do. Who is the despairing individual proclaiming such a seemingly hopeless state? The writer of this book is the self-titled "Qoheleth," which is a Hebrew title meaning something like "teacher," "speaker," or "preacher." The one who teaches the perceived gloom and doom—at turns a theistic, nihilistic, and existentialist prophet-teacher-philosopher-poet—has been branded as a melancholy thinker who surveys life and sees nothing but vanity, uselessness, nothingness. Qoheleth recalls the wise king Solomon and creates a Solomon-like persona in order to establish his wisdom credentials. Even so, the poor man's proclamation is often considered borderline heterodoxy. Heterodoxy is a combination of heresy and unorthodoxy. We can't have such stuff in the Bible, can we? So, you see why many a well-intentioned commentator, wishing to contain this mischievous thorn in the side of traditional Jewish interpretation and palatable Christian thought, has portrayed Qoheleth as the antithesis of everything else contained in Scripture. If we need a nice philosophical syllogism where A + B must always equal C, then this would be enough. But maybe Qoheleth is suggesting that A + B must not always equal C. And if so, then maybe we need to reconsider some of what we think we know about the God who Jesus called Father.

So Qoheleth remains in the Tanakh and the Christian canon, but because of the very presence of Ecclesiastes, there will be many difficulties in interpretation. The predominant presuppositions that have emerged as primary in the book's interpretation have shaped the preponderance of perception for centuries. We mostly have Jerome, Origen, and various church fathers to thank for the traditional understandings of Ecclesiastes we may have become accustomed to. And these early Christian thinkers were heavily influenced by several interpretive moves in the Targum, which was an ancient paraphrase of Hebrew Scripture rendered in the more-popular spoken Aramaic of first-century Palestine. Many of the issues debated throughout the last two millennia deal with things like Solomonic authorship, the theme of the book—whether "vanity of vanities," the quest for joy, the *summum bonum*, which is the ultimate goal of life, etc.—and the varying degrees of tension in Ecclesiastes have set the tone for the history of Qoheleth exegesis. But could it be that many of these tacts—both Jewish and Christian—are attempts to re-interpret Qoheleth by reading what is not there? Or by reading what is only there on the surface? This Qoheleth must be dealt with on the terms in the text, the context, and the wisdom literature co-text. And though he must be dealt with in his historical trajectory, he must also be considered in conjunction with what comes after him and with the full range of what we have come to know or think we have come to know. There are no other terms. What is this poet who dares color outside the lines trying to communicate? Perhaps our emphasis should be on the questions Qoheleth asks. If so, we may see that we continue to wrestle with the same questions today. Then we must decide what to do with these questions.

We might gather that Ecclesiastes remains a book of the Bible today because it at least says something about the God of Israel, wisdom, and the goal of life, even if what it seems to be saying on the surface does not mingle well with what the rest of Scripture says. Maybe that's part of the reasoning. Or maybe our ancient spiritual ancestors from different ages and differing theologies have been brave enough to recognize the elephant in the room of Christian thought. And maybe they suspected that this elephant wasn't an elephant at all. What I mean is, maybe Ecclesiastes has more to tell us than we can easily glean from it at first look. That's what the rest of this book will grapple with. I will attempt to make this journey through the looking-glass of Ecclesiastes as pleasant, engaging, and even fun as possible. This will not be a straightforward commentary. This will not be rote textual exegesis. This will not be a theological tome. This will not be a philosophical treatise. All of these things will play a part in this exploration, but we will also encounter poetry, drama, meditation, and self-reflection. And in this process, even when we face difficult questions, even when we are challenged to rethink our assumptions, even when we are faced with things that don't fit easily into some modern-day Christian thinking, we might discover that Qoheleth has many of the same fears, joys, questions, and responses that we have. If so, we might take a small step toward becoming more human, more like reflections of Christ, more like the people God dreams for us to be. We might find out that the elephant in the room was just waiting to be introduced properly, and once we get to know it, we realize it never was an elephant after all.

1

The Usefulness of Uselessness

But there is nothing useless in nature, not even uselessness itself.
—MICHEL DE MONTAIGNE

WHEN I WAS A young boy, I used to shoot the basketball from my chest. I would heave the ball from my chest into the air, fervently hoping the ball would get over the front of that rim and into the basket. My body was still developing, and that ten-foot hoop was so high up there. A shot heaved from my chest was my only shot at making, well, a shot. My form was preliminary, developing, nascent. My content was the occasional made basketball shot. As I grew, I began shooting from just above my right shoulder. And I saw a few more shots regularly go in the basket. In my high school years, I was able to mimic the form of professional basketball players by beginning my shot with the ball over my head. Finally, as a senior in high school, I could make more shots using good basketball form. Throughout all these variations of form, my content was incrementally different, somewhat better. And my form had evolved to be almost identical to professional ball players. My form suggested that

I should be making the majority of the shots I attempted. But I could never make fifty shots in a row like Larry Bird.

Nevertheless, there was some congruity between the growth of my form and the growth of my content related to basketball. That's generally what we expect in all things in life. We expect that form and content will closely coincide. We see the form of a red stop light, and we expect to see all the vehicles near and facing that light to be stopped. We see four walls and a roof, and we anticipate that this is a structure of a house, or a shop, or a storage facility. We see six chairs gathered around a table, and we are confident that there are meals shared by family and friends around this table. Perhaps we are so accustomed to content necessarily following form that we are hard-pressed to imagine it being any other way. But Qoheleth does. Do we have eyes to see what Qoheleth sees?

We are modern people who crave usefulness and efficacy. We want, say, a fork to behave like a fork. We want it to pierce the crisp lettuce leaves of a salad and hold them temporarily on its tines as the delicious greenery is transferred to our waiting mouths. We want the side of that fork to efficiently slice through most foods as we slightly wiggle it from the top of our chosen cuisine right through the bottom to the plate. We are so tuned into the usefulness of a fork that we would consider it foolish to use a fork to eat soup. We might consider someone who laboriously made their way through a cup of soup with a fork a bit off, or incredibly strange at least. No, we are confident that forks are for salads and spoons are for soups. To trade the one for the other and expect the same usefulness would be foolish. It might be considered uselessness. In Qoheleth's vernacular, we might call it vanity. What is this vanity he espouses and derides?

I've raised two questions near the beginning of this chapter that need some investigating. And at first, the questions may not seem related. For the sake of clarity, allow me to pose these questions succinctly again:

1. Does content match form in Ecclesiastes?

2. What is the vanity that Qoheleth so often speaks of in the book of Ecclesiastes?

These questions are not only important in considering this one book in Scripture; they also concern the whole of human history. For if we find that sometimes form and content are incongruent, then we must admit there are some things we don't yet know. What's more, there are some things that we think we know, but must confess we might be wrong about. Also, if vanity turns out to be something other than uselessness, wind, breath, meaning-lessness, and emptiness, then we must admit that there might be something beyond our perceived nothingness. Is all that clear as mud? Good. Let's look at these questions a little more.

Form and Content

What does Qoheleth have to say about the relationship between form and content? As I mentioned above, there has long been a persistent influence of the foundational understanding that form and content are synonymous. We can see this in the field of literary forms, where we often perceive some of what the content will be, simply by recognizing the form.

Consider a poem. If a certain poem has fourteen lines, and the rhyme scheme is made up of three quatrains followed by a couplet, then we can be certain we are reading a Shakespearean sonnet. Further, this form almost always uses the first twelve lines to explore some setting, or character, or relationship in a way that persuades us into agreeing with the line of thought. Then in the final two lines, the whole trajectory swerves in a surprising or un-expected direction. The content follows the form, and the form dictates what the content will be.

Or consider a script for the stage. If we see "Act 1" as a head-ing at the very beginning of the text, we know this is a play. This is further supported by the distinctive device of character names preceding what those characters say. And if we see one character name, then we generally expect to see at least one other name of an additional character. We know that dialogue will carry much of the content of this type of writing.

Analyzing form is one of the major ways that literary critics—and we lowly readers—access the meaning of a text. So, when we turn to the book of Ecclesiastes, it would be nice to find a litany of aphorisms, similar to much of Proverbs. Then we would know that this is a text that will mainly be offering wisdom and prudent guidance. Qoheleth gives us some aphorisms, but that's not all. It might be nice to find chiastic poems (poems with a structure involving the second half mirroring or reflecting the first half). Then we would know that this might be some type of story condensed into lyric form. Qoheleth gives us some of this kind of poetry, but that's not all. It might be nice to find inverted liturgies. Then we would know we are starting with a general theme and moving toward something specific. Qoheleth gives us some of these liturgies, but that's not all. Are you noticing a pattern? Let's cut to the chase then. The only pattern in Ecclesiastes is the lack of literary pattern. There is no coherent structure. The text, as a whole, suggests an incoherent litany of questions with no satisfactory answers.

So, if form and content go together, then one would think that the disjointed structure of Ecclesiastes yields a confusing incoherency. If the literary form is all over the place, then we can't get much of a consistent message from Ecclesiastes, right? Well—Martin Heidegger, that brilliant, yet obtuse and obfuscating, German philosopher of the twentieth century, insisted that form is equal in meaning to content. Always. A quick read of the first three chapters of Ecclesiastes would cause even the fledgling philosophy student to throw shade at the accomplished Heidegger on this point. Qoheleth, the passionate, orthodox, non-conformist sage will not give us a form that coheres with its content. Much commentary over the last half century attempts to assimilate the scattered and dissimilar form and content of Ecclesiastes, insisting that structure, form, and meaning go together. But such statements reveal a bias toward Heidegger. No, rather form and function in this book could not be more contradictory. In fact, the meaning might be crystallized by the disjointed form. With stops and starts that at turns laud and question the traditional wisdom understandings, a new—i.e., reimagined—vision of sense is taking shape.

Uselessness

So is there anything consistent in Qoheleth's unorganized and seemingly rambling diatribe? Yes: *hebel*. This is the leitmotif of Qoheleth's questioning, and runs through the fabric of the entire book. The emergence of his new vision of sense starts with *hebel*. So what is *hebel*? This Hebrew term has something to do with each of the following: uselessness, nothing, meaninglessness, emptiness, vanity, breath. In the defining cry of Qoheleth's work, we see *hebel* repeated five times: "'*Hebel* of *hebels*,' says the Teacher, '*hebel* of *hebels*! All is *hebel*'" (1:2). That is to say, "Vanity of vanities, vanity of vanities! All is vanity." Or, if you like, "Uselessness of uselessness! All is useless." Or, "Emptiness of emptiness! All is emptiness." Or even, "Meaninglessness of all meaninglessness, meaninglessness of all meaninglessness! All is meaningless." Or, if you really want to get literal, "Vapor of vapors! All is vapor." And finally, for the very picky literalist, "Mist of mists! All is mist."

Quick note on translation: if you're looking for the definitive definition of *hebel*, you won't find it here. Like most of the imaginative and porous ancient Hebrew language, this word and term can have multiple meanings and varied levels of nuance. As an example, in the closing verses of Proverbs (just one page away from the beginning of Ecclesiastes in most any Bible), beauty is described as *hebel*. In this usage, it seems to suggest that beauty doesn't last. Then in the very opening of his text, Qoheleth describes everything as *hebel*. I've yet to find an English translation that uses the same word for *hebel* in these two verses.

Now, back to *hebel*. Is this *hebel* the only thing consistent about Qoheleth's narrative? This emptiness? This uselessness? Is he really just the pessimistic skeptic that rejects any meaning?

Here's a better question: Why is the honest recognition of meaninglessness considered pessimistic? You see, we must recognize that the situations Qoheleth describes as *hebel* are circumstances that occur in his world, in a specific time and place. These disturbing situations raise serious theological questions about God's activity—or lack thereof—in the world, in a specific time and place. The unanswered questions, the enigmatic mysteries of life, the attempts at the impossible; they are observed for what they are, and Qoheleth still urges that the listening community enjoy life. Thus, Qoheleth's use of *hebel* appears to be different from its normal Old Testament usage, usually meaning *vapor, vanity,* or *worthlessness.* There does seem to be an element of nothingness to this *hebel.* However, it is a nothingness that is the process, or even conclusion, of anything severed from the life of God: life that is to be enjoyed. So, is the thematic unity of this book something more than a nihilistic, empty nothingness?

A Quick Theological Sketch

To get a sense of the unusual relationship between form and content, and to understand uselessness a bit better, I ask your indulgence for a short overview of the book of Ecclesiastes. The lens through which we will view Qoheleth's thought is a theological one. There are a few reasons for choosing theology as what will shape the following sketch:

- First, the book is included in the sacred texts of two major religions: Judaism and Christianity. Therefore, it must be approached as having at least some small thing to do with how we think about divinity.

- Second, a strict literary overview would be intriguing, but might miss some of what Qoheleth is suggesting and questioning, since he himself mentions God several times.

- Third, only by considering theological aspects of Qoheleth's writing can we allow ourselves to be uncomfortable with theological things: a practice I believe to be necessary. This is an argument I'll wrestle with at other places in this book.

- And finally, I am a theological being. That is to say, the primary trajectory of my thought is a combination of artistic, philosophical, and theological concerns. To negate theological considerations is to negate some part of myself. So, as I am the one writing this book, we will consider Ecclesiastes theologically.

Qoheleth seems to be obsessed with three primary questions:

1. Is there anything to be gained from our work?

2. Is there anything new under the sun?

3. What is the purpose of wisdom?

His concern with these three questions is woven throughout the fabric of all he writes, observes, and wonders about. These three questions are actually dimensions of a bigger question: What is the purpose of this life? Qoheleth has a burning desire, after years of *hebel*, to wrestle with this question. In his search, he consistently refers to a lasting gain: "What do people gain from all the toil at which they toil under the sun?" (1:3). This "gain" is the Hebrew term *yithron*, occurring ten times in Ecclesiastes (1:3; 2:11, 13, 22; 3:9; 5:9, 16; 7:12; 10:10, 11), with participial and adverbial forms occurring elsewhere (2:15; 6:8, 11; 7:11, 16; 12:9, 12). And Qoheleth raises further questions about this gain. Is it something that can be earned? Or is it received as a gift?

In the prologue of the book, there is abundant activity. This is evidenced by the plethora of active participles utilized in 1:4–8. However, this torrent of motion achieves nothing: *hebel*. Every word and image is wearisome. If there is a purpose to this life, it must be contained within some ancient purpose for "there is nothing new under the sun" (1:9). Of course, Qoheleth turns right around and questions this very declaration he has just made: can anything be said to be new? Qoheleth clearly sees the ease with which humanity deems old things new. The everlasting sameness cannot be affected even by traditional wisdom. The task of attempting to understand the world is by no means easy: "it is an unhappy business that God has given to human beings to be busy with." "Unhappy" here is the Hebrew term *ra'*, in context meaning not so much "evil" as "painful." This is an understanding that stems from Genesis 3:17, wherein the man must begin to toil in order to eat. Yet Qoheleth does not resign himself to a life of pity in his toil, however *ra'* it may be. Rather, he plunges into a quest full of questions.

Throughout chapter 2, Qoheleth remembers various approaches in his search. The indulgence in fleeting pleasure ends unsatisfactorily (2:1–11). Qoheleth's conclusion? There is no *yithron* in the accomplishments of space and time in and of themselves (2:11). Even a turn to the sapiential framework—which points the way to *yithron* more so than does folly (2:13)—is, in the end, *hebel*. Even more, to toil with wisdom and knowledge is a great *ra'* if sought for its own benefit (2:21). At the end of this section, Qoheleth lays out his theological basis for God's gift of life that is intended for humanity's enjoyment:

> The greatest good for humanity is to eat and drink and discover life's delight amid their toil. I perceived this also is God's gift; for outside him who can eat, who can have satisfaction? (Eccl 2:24–25, my translation)

This major matter of God's gift intended for enjoyment, delight, satisfaction, repeats throughout the book (3:12, 22; 5:18; 8:15; 9:7–10). Is this gift freely given to all humanity? Or only to "the one who pleases him" (2:26)? The amazing reality that Qoheleth observes is not that God picks and chooses on whom to bestow the gift of satisfaction-filled life; but rather that the onus for discovering delight in life is on those who respond to the gift by cooperating in the work God has laid out for humanity by eating, drinking, and pursuing enjoyment as God has intended.

I am aware that this is in stark contrast to the making of "many books"—of which "there is no end" (12:12)—which clearly delineate God's giving as arbitrary. For example: "God gives as God pleases, and there is no consistency that Qoheleth can discover about this 'giving'; it is mystery, rather than generosity."[1] Also,

> Human life and action pale against the work of the eternal, immutable God. God's plans are irrevocable and no one can alter them. They must be accepted on their own

---

1. Murphy, *Tree of Life*, 54.

terms; hence, Qoheleth's advice is to welcome both toil
and joy within life's ever-changing rhythms.[2]

In response to the first quote about the lack of consistency,
Qoheleth discovers that the arbitrariness is not in God's giving of
the gift, but in humanity's acceptance. As for the second quote's
assurance of what God is like, Qoheleth does not see an immutable
God behind nor above this ever-changing world. Remember that
Qoheleth is within the school of wisdom that sees the creator-God
and his creation connected. If the rhythms of life are in constant
flux, then this speaks something to the God in whose life humanity knows it is contained. Perhaps the foil to inconsistent interpretation is provided in the following hermeneutical statement on
Ecclesiastes: "Either there is no God, or all that is and happens is
a moment in the being and life of God . . . who is identical with
the world."[3] The sap of every present moment most be drained as
God's gift. And it is a gift that comes from a creator who continually interacts with creation in surprising ways.

Qoheleth makes a move to reflect on the nature of time in
chapter 3, and he does this in poetic fashion. The chiastic structure of this poem, of the times appointed to every event, gives
the impression that God has given his human creation a glimpse
of all that transcends time and space. This points to the inter-
section of "gain"—*yithron*—the "best thing"—*tob*—and "gift"—
mattath—held in tension in the passage of 3:9–15. I dig deeper
into this passage in chapter 7 of this book, where we engage in a
pursuit of what is hidden.

Thematic emphasis of the oppressed, envy of another's work,
companionship, and the interplay of wisdom and politics are woven
throughout chapters 4 and 5. The outstanding feature of this section
is Qoheleth's bold statement on worship. In uncharacteristic fashion
for sapiential material, Qoheleth radically situates a life of doxol-
ogy in the miasma of dreams, mysteries, and words that he observes
under the sun (5:7). The one before whom we can say nothing and

---

2. Brown, *Character in Crisis*, 145.

3. Delitzsch, *Proverbs, Ecclesiastes*, 179.

yet contains all in his own life, is the one to whom we must respond with reverence and awe. This worship is linked to the end of chapter 5, where humans are observed "to accept their lot and find enjoyment in their toil—this is the gift of God" (5:19). The concept of *yithron* crystallizes into an acceptance or reception of the gift of life in God. Yes, everything under the sun—outside the life of God—is *hebel*. But to those who eat and drink and find enjoyment in life's toil, Qoheleth has discovered this "to be good" (5:18).

Chapters 6, 7, and 8 are a jumbling of the issues and pursuits in life that end in *hebel*, with Qoheleth's proverbial advice on various points. The entire section ends with the repeated summating call to the best thing: delight in the good gift of life (8:15). There is intriguing symmetry between the litany contained in 7:1–9 and wisdom in the flesh when Christ speaks blessings and woes in Luke 6:20–26. Indeed, blessing and curse are accepted as necessary and integral aspects of this life: "In the day of prosperity be joyful, and in the day of adversity consider; God has made the one as well as the other, so that mortals may not find out anything that will come after them" (Eccl 7:14). This perspective keeps humans rooted in the present, so that they may have full opportunity to receive the life gifted them in enjoyment. The good intent of God as creator is clearly defined and juxtaposed with the perversion of that intent by his own creation: "See, this alone I found, that God made human beings, straightforward, but they have devised many schemes" (7:29). This point is revisited in 8:12, where the responsibility of *ra'* is placed on humanity, not on God: "Though sinners do evil a hundred times." The phrases "God made" of 7:29 and the "sinners do" of 8:12 are the same verb, namely *'asah*—meaning to do or make something with specific action. The good action of God is perverted by the bad action of humanity. Qoheleth does not grant moral evil any ontological purchase.

The investigation of wisdom becomes intense in chapters 9, 10, and 11. Though wisdom be powerful and stronger than folly (9:13–18), limitations to wisdom remain (11:1–6). Uniquely, Qoheleth is calling the listener to particular courses of action: "Send out your bread" (11:1); "sow your seed" (11:6); "Follow the inclination of your heart and the desire of your eyes" (11:9); and "Banish anxiety" (11:10). And the supreme call is to "Remember your creator" (12:1). Immediately, our minds might turn to the story of God as narrated in the Genesis account: creator, gift, joy, and toil are woven together there as well. Qoheleth's eyes have been wide open to all the *hebel* he has discovered. Yet in the midst of this world of uselessness, God gifts us with joy in life's toil. Qoheleth is reimagining the wisdom tradition and threading a dramatically coherent view of a God who is enigmatic, yet still creating life as a gift.

Finally, we come to the epilogue of Ecclesiastes in 12:9–13. It seems to me this was not originally what Qoheleth penned. I suspect some well-meaning editors came along and tried to tie up some loose ends to make Ecclesiastes more palatable. We tend to do that. We think we know so much, and so when something messes with our notions of control, we re-narrate what seems out of step. Greater minds than mine may come to a different conclusion. All I know is those final verses seem forced onto what Qoheleth has questioned and investigated. Read it for yourself, and see what you think.

And here concludes this theological sketch. It will be all too brief for some. It will be too shallow for others, just scratching the surface of what is there. It will be far too wordy and laden with Hebrew terms for some. It will be too philosophical and unnecessarily provocative for others. I say with great fervor that I agree with all those opinions and more. Hopefully it raises at least one question for each reader; a question which cannot be easily dismissed nor readily answered; a question that must be lived with and wrestled with and argued with. If I accomplish that, I would consider it an honor to Qoheleth's legacy of questioning.

2

A Brief History of Questioning

What can one say when one admits one knows nothing?
—SOCRATES IN PLATO'S *EUTHYPHRO*

Consider these questions:

- What is piety?
- What is impiety?
- Is piety always the same in every action?
- What sort of difference creates enmity?
- Is an object of love in a state of becoming or suffering?
- Should we accept the opinion of the majority?
- Is a good decision based on knowledge or something else?
- When a person considers applying a medicine to their eyes, is that person consulting about the medicine or about the eyes?
- What is the nature of virtue?

- How does courage enable a soldier to fight at his post, yet also enable another soldier to flee?

- Is courage noble?

- How do we discern if someone possesses the quality of temperance?

- Is temperance to be considered good?

- How do you know who you are?

- What is justice?

- Is there such a thing as absolute justice?

- Is that which is beautiful and good also necessarily true?

- In what qualities are bees alike, rather than different from each other?

- Is virtue the same in a child as in a parent?

- Does someone who desires what is honorable also desire what is good?

I could sit with just one or two of these questions for hours. Some of the questions would consume a lifetime and never be exhaustively addressed. The above list of questions is just a tiny sampling of questions from Socrates as recorded in the dramatic dialogues of his student, Plato. There are thousands upon thousands of questions that Socrates posed in these works. Now, we know that the extant writings we have today are not from Socrates himself. And we have no idea how much literary license Plato took in writing down these dialogues between Socrates and others. And there are epistemologists—learned academics who study how we know what we know—who will tell us that we cannot really know anything from the supposed questions of Socrates because the texts themselves are suspect, or we don't really know how much of what is recorded was actually spoken by Socrates, and so on, and so on. Hogwash! Whether Socrates was real, or whether any of these dialogues actually occurred, or whether Plato made everything up—all of that makes for some diverting historical speculation, but none of it has anything to do with what we can know.

The questions of Socrates that stem from four centuries before Christ are so pervasive in the western world that today, some 2,500 years later, we still refer to them in our modes of education! We have things like Socratic questions and Socratic seminars. These monikers reference a type of questioning that gets at, not so much what we know, but what we think we know and how we come to know it. In fact, our best educational practices have more to do with questions than answers, in that we teach students how to ask questions in such a way that they learn how to learn. When a student masters how to learn, then she can learn anything.

If you happen to not be that familiar with the questions of Socrates in Plato's dialogues, you might think that every single one of Socrates' questions are profound and cannot be answered with a simple *yes* or *no*. But it is his persistent method of questioning that is profound; the sheer volume of questions, not just their content. He has been called the "Gadfly of Athens" because of his inexhaustible ability to seemingly ask a barrage of unending questions. Consider my version of a section of the dialogue between Socrates and Meno below.

SOCRATES:

If virtue is knowledge, can virtue be taught?

MENO

Certainly.

SOCRATES

So then, if virtue is of such a nature as knowledge, it will be taught; and if not, not?

MENO
Indeed.

SOCRATES

The next question is, whether virtue is knowledge or of another species?

MENO

Yes, that appears to be the question which comes next.

SOCRATES

Do we not say that virtue is good?

MENO

Certainly.

SOCRATES

Now, if there be any sort of good which is distinct from knowledge, virtue may be that good; but if knowledge embraces all good, then we shall be right to think that virtue is knowledge?

MENO

True.

SOCRATES

And virtue makes us good?

MENO

Yes.

SOCRATES

And if we are good, then we are profitable; for all good things are profitable?

MENO

Yes.

SOCRATES

Then virtue is profitable?

MENO

That is the only inference possible.

SOCRATES

Then, now let us see what are the things which may profit us. Health and strength, and beauty and wealth: these, and things like them, we call profitable?

MENO

True.

SOCRATES

And yet these things may also sometimes do us harm: would you not think so?

MENO

Yes.

SOCRATES

And what is the guiding principle which makes them profitable or the reverse? Are they not profitable when they are rightly used, and hurtful when they are not rightly used?

MENO

Certainly.

SOCRATES

Next, let us consider the goods of the soul: they are temperance, justice, courage, understanding, memory, generosity, and the like?

MENO

Surely.

SOCRATES

And such of these as are not knowledge, but of another sort, are sometimes profitable and sometimes hurtful; as, for example, courage without prudence, which is only a sort of confidence? As in, when a man has no sense he is harmed by courage, but when he has sense he is profited?

MENO

True.

SOCRATES

And the same may be said of temperance and understanding; whatever things are learned or done with sense are profitable, but when done without sense they are hurtful?

MENO

Very true.

SOCRATES

And in general, all that endures, when under the guidance of wisdom, ends in happiness; but when under the guidance of folly, in the opposite?

MENO

That appears to be true.

SOCRATES

If then virtue is a quality of the soul, and is admitted to be profitable, it must be wisdom or prudence, since none of the things of the soul are either profitable or hurtful in themselves, but they are all made profitable or hurtful by the addition of wisdom or of folly; and, therefore, if virtue is profitable, virtue must be a sort of wisdom or prudence?

MENO

I quite agree.

SOCRATES

And the other goods, such as wealth and the like, of which we were just now saying that they are sometimes good and sometimes evil, do not they also become profitable or hurtful accordingly as the soul guides and uses them rightly or wrongly; just as the things of the soul are benefited when under the guidance of wisdom and harmed by folly?

MENO

True.

SOCRATES

And the wise soul guides them rightly, and the foolish soul wrongly?

MENO

Yes.

SOCRATES

And is not this universally true of human nature? All other things hang upon the soul, and the things of the soul hang upon wisdom, if they are to be good; and so wisdom is inferred to be that which profits and virtue, as we say, is profitable?

MENO

Certainly.

SOCRATES

And thus we arrive at the conclusion that virtue is either wholly or partly wisdom?

MENO

I think that what you are saying, Socrates, is very true.

∽

Relentless! Meno—and so many other of Socrates' conversation partners—seemed to display far more patience than I would.

By the seventh or eighth question, I'd insist that Socrates get on to his point: "Say what you want to say already!" And therein is the problem. Maybe we seek answers far too readily and far too often. Socrates' whole point may simply be the question; or the litany of questions. He may already be saying what he wants to say with each question. Notice how every time he speaks in the above excerpt it is always with a question. He makes no definitive statements except as a result of Meno's answers and as part of a succeeding question.

It could be argued that the whole history of human questioning lies in the shadow of Socrates and his ocean of questions. Roughly the same time as Plato was creating dramatic dialogues with Socrates as the star questioner, somewhere in a post-exilic Hebrew remnant, someone with the title of Qoheleth took up the mantle of questioning and gave us Ecclesiastes. And we still wrestle with the questions of Socrates and Qoheleth today. We struggle with the inquiries of Jesus and Cicero. We have no easy answers for the examinations of Augustine and Hildegard von Bingen. We are still overwhelmed with investigations from the likes of Shakespeare, Erasmus, Kierkegaard, Martin Luther, Nietzsche, Chesterton, Woolf, Camus, and so many other great questioners.

Like Socrates, like Qoheleth, we may be well served to spend more time sitting with the groundswell of questions that life brings, rather than pouring our time and resources into discovering definitive answers. And maybe we should pay more than lip-service to such a quest. In education arenas, Socratic questioning is lauded by the same bureaucracy that could never conceive of a student's mastery of Socratic questioning to be a measure of knowledge. No, we would rather see a high percentile on a multiple-choice test. A test where the ratio of answers to questions is at least four to one. Maybe we are surrounded by too many potential answers and have ignored the endless sea of questions long enough. Or, perhaps we have tried to move on from the questions far too quickly.

In a document of only about 4,500 words, Qoheleth gives us over forty-five questions. That's one question for every hundred words! Seems reminiscent of Socrates, doesn't it? And what's more,

Qoheleth isn't trying to give definitive answers to the questions he raises. In fact, it can be argued that the only satisfactory answer that Qoheleth gives to all of his questions is the most enigmatic: It's all useless, because "all is vanity." And therein may be a clue for us. Perhaps the usefulness of uselessness comes in unexpectedly. Because we may discern that answers are useless. But in reaching that conclusion, we find the great potential and possibility in the usefulness of questions. The nothingness is the answer we so readily try to hold on to. But there is something beyond all that nothingness, and it's what was granted to us at the start: the question.

What if we followed Qoheleth's lead and focused on questions more than answers? What if we followed Socrates in being at home with questions? What if we valued the usefulness of questions over and above the seeming uselessness of solid answers? What if journeys were more important than destinations to us? What if our discomfort with uncertainty, like what I'm suggesting, stems from our need to be in control? And what if we focused on creating rather than control?

Let's sit with this last question for a moment. Just as a brief example, we might take a cue from Qoheleth and consider the possibility that God, on purpose, intended for us to be wildly imaginative creators who could persevere and create something even when we are out of control. Why do I think this? Because that's how God creates.

There is a theological theory many are familiar with called *creatio ex nihilo*. This theory posits that God created with no material, God created out of nothing. This theory has been assimilated into doctrine, and is predicated on English translations of the first lines of the book of Genesis in Hebrew Scripture. Here are a few English translations of part of Genesis 1:2, the verse in question:

- "The earth was formless and empty, and darkness covered the deep waters" (NLT);

- "The earth was a formless void and darkness covered the face of the deep" (NRSV);

- "Now the earth was formless and empty, darkness was over the surface of the deep" (NIV);

- "The earth was formless and void, and darkness was over the surface of the deep" (NASB).

The Hebrew words that are translated variously above as "formless," "empty," or "void" are *tohu wa-bohu*. This is not Qoheleth's *hebel*. Yet, this phrase is also difficult to translate because it is a bit of Hebrew wordplay. Eastern European languages have translated this phrase to mean "confusion" or "commotion." The basic idea that the Hebrew writer is trying to get across is that there is some sort of unshakable, confused matter over which the Spirit of God is hovering. No one can shape this! No one can bring order out of this chaos. No one can color this void. Except the right kind of creator. God speaks and this unshaped and unshapeable confusion is ordered, aligned, and created into something beautiful.

God is this kind of creator. A creator who takes whatever is available, even a formless void, an apparent nothingness, and creates something extraordinary. But if the creator is God and has ultimate control, couldn't God just change the material God works with? If so, why doesn't God do that? Maybe God's control is something we've misunderstood.

Granted that attempts to describe God are flawed from the start. After all, we are human. We are not divine. But, if God chose to control the creative process and all its implications, then God would not finish the creative process until God has all the right materials and has a finished product that is perfect. And yet, throughout thousands of years of humans on earth, there is very little, if any, perfection going on. Maybe God doesn't mind using imperfection and failure as materials in God's creative process. And instead of arguing for *creatio ex nihilo* from the Genesis text, we might consider the logic flawed. If so, we'd have to look at something like the resurrection of Christ to begin to explain new creation that comes out of nothingness. But that is for another book.

See what happens when we dare to question and sit with the questions? We may not find answers. But the time spent living in the questions is rarely time wasted. In chapters 3, 4, and 5 of this book, we'll look at Qoheleth's primary three questions in a creative way. At other places in this book you'll find slightly more direct ways to address those same three questions. But if a creative God, a questioning Socrates, and an enigmatic Qoheleth teach us anything, perhaps it is this: the direct approach is seldom the most beautiful.

Interlude

God the Weaver

WHAT IS GOD LIKE?

Sometimes I imagine God as a Weaver.

An old lady. Ancient. Timeless. Sitting at her loom.

Her hands wrinkled and bent from centuries of weaving.

Her eyes meticulously scanning the warp and weft of her current project.

She is not picky about the materials she weaves.

Scattered around her feet are yarns, silks, and fabrics. But there also are leaves, vines, ripped clothing, various textiles. Some beam with the brightness of their hue; others fade into the confusion of dullness that is the dusty, wooden floor.

As the ancient Weaver completes a line of warp—the strand so taut an observer might guess its snapping is imminent—she bends down, slowly, steadily stooping to collect in her deformed (yet amazingly gentle) hands a new strand.

She is surprised to clasp a bit of husky vine. No matter that the strand before was pure silk. She has a way of weaving together the sublime and the pedestrian into magnificent forms and patterns.

God the Weaver loves this kind of surprise.

God the Weaver takes the challenge into herself and fashions beauty out of broken and ugly material.

This timeless Weaver is a master of the heddles on the loom, able to move her stuff into seemingly impossible right angles. Yes, it is her stuff. In some mysterious way, it is as if the weave originated from her own being.

No matter the source material, it bears her likeness. And with this material that is her very own, she creates space for the new, the old, the surprising.

God the Weaver takes time in her craft, methodically filling the loom with wonder and eagerly anticipating the end design.

3

Into the Woods with Kierkegaard and Erasmus

What do people gain from all their toil under the sun?

—QOHELETH

HE WAS OFTEN A midnight walker through these woods. A few meters from his back porch presented a tangled wood of hard-won paths, crudely fashioned by his own axe and heavy boots. Years ago, there was no discernible path in or through this forest. Now there were many. His own feet had tramped down the underbrush, over days, weeks, decades. His own axe had been worn down by the dozens of saplings he'd sacrificed over what seemed like a lifetime. Their felling had meant a new crook in the path, a surprising detour to the stream, a slight diversion around the grander and older trunks that had themselves once been saplings years ago, centuries, eons.

Now as he walked these familiar paths again, for the thousandth time and for the first, his inner monologue carried his thoughts far away from this wood at the midnight hour. Or was it a dialogue? Alone in his long periods of solitude, he had enjoyed many a conversation with fresh characters: Niels Klim, Margarete, Constantin Constantius, Johannes the Seducer. He had also argued with those partial reflections of himself: Climacus, anti-Climacus, and Johannes de Silencio. Fragments of philosophical wanderings and wonderings were fleshing themselves out in his mind. Kingdoms were being felled, just like the young trees that once stood where he now trod. At the wake of empires fallen, he was composing postscripts and editorial comments.

"What is truth but to live for an idea," he thought. And the reply came to him easily.

"Truth is subjectivity," quipped Climacus.

"Ah, yes. But subjectivity is also truth," he continued.

"Are you saying that truth cannot be absolute?" asked Margarete.

"Only if all ulterior motives for seeking and knowing and experiencing truth can be eliminated, or at least relegated."

"But such a project is implausible, perhaps even impossible," interjected Johannes de Silencio.

"Then I repeat: subjectivity is truth."

The cacophony of voices flowed in and out of each other seamlessly. For they were all his voice. That is not to say he struggled with multiple personalities, nor that his mind was divided. Rather, that he found the portioning of dialogue within himself to be convincing. Maybe even normal. This inner construction of a self-made community was certainly more conducive to working out the practicality of theoretical initiatives than was the futile exercise of trying to dialogue with the power players of the religious institution. Each time he tried, it was like banging his head against a wall. He came away from the conflict bleeding and bruised with a nasty headache, and the church system continued in its ignorance undeterred. If a Protestant was marked by his or her singular insistence on ever and always protesting, then Soren Kierkegaard was the exemplary definition of one.

"Yes, the subjectivity of truth is what makes it true," he continued. "It is in the subjective experience of what is true that truth must, and can only, be realized."

He was about to add that truth must seek an appropriate relation between knower and object when an unfamiliar voice chimed in with a rejoinder. "But what type of knowledge is the knower seeking? You must acquire the best knowledge first," said the voice.

"That wasn't me," he thought.

"Correct," said the voice.

Ah, so he had spoken it, not thought it. Well, this was often the case during his walks in the woods. But now, startled at the sound of a voice emanating from somewhere outside himself, he stopped still, peered in the direction of the voice and saw, propped against a tree to his left, just off the path, what seemed to be a bear with a man's head.

"What are you?" he asked.

"*What*, Soren? Do you not mean to say, *who*?"

Ah, just a man in a fur coat. Not the impossibility of a man-headed bear this night.

"Fine. Who then? And how do you come to know my name?" he asked.

"Perhaps the more pressing question is how do I come to find myself in a wood in Denmark out of my time?" said the man.

Soren considered this perplexing question, realizing immediately that it required the consideration of other questions first before properly returning to address it. Such is the nature of good questions. "May I take that phrase 'out of my time' to mean temporal issues are at play in our meeting? No, don't answer that first. Start with 'who.'"

"Very well then. Desiderius Erasmus. Of Rotterdam."

"Dutch! Of course. Interjecting themselves where they are not invited is a distinctively damnable Dutch trait," said Soren.

"So you have labeled us all, then have you?" teased Erasmus.

"Not at all. A matter of opinion."

"Of prejudice. In the country of the blind, the one-eyed man is king."

"Conceded. Of Rotterdam you say?"

"Yes. But I have been a wandering scholar. Beyond my homeland, I know England, Italy, and France well," Erasmus answered.

"And obviously this wood in Denmark. I myself have never left Copenhagen."

"No, you never did."

"Never will, you mean?"

Erasmus addressed this question indirectly, "Soren, this is my first time in this wood, and I am some three centuries your predecessor."

Soren held his breath. Strange though this assertion was, it was not unexpected. He exhaled. A long relinquishing of sense that simultaneously accepted Erasmus' truth.

"I have been walking this wood for what seems one eternal midnight," said Soren.

"Tonight we are citizens of the world, known to all, and to all, strangers," Erasmus pontificated.

"So this is . . . ?" He trailed off, unsure how to marry his theology with this reality in a concise and coherent statement. This might have been the first time he had ever been at a loss for words.

Erasmus noted the sudden silence. He inhaled deeply and slowly turned his gaze upward. Through the bramble of ancient boughs, the full moon's light glistened on this cold winter night. A faint smile formed at the corner of Erasmus' mouth. "This is simply a walk in the woods," he finally said. "And having never met you, I find myself knowing you."

"Let us walk then. Join me."

Erasmus stepped onto the path, and the two men walked together in silence for a few moments. Suddenly, Soren felt a wave of remembrance rush over him. This was Erasmus of Rotterdam. Of course. The erstwhile inspirer of Martin Luther who would become one of Luther's greatest critics and debaters. Yes, in fact Erasmus never joined the Reformation!

Soren began to feel aftershocks of all his collisions with Christendom over the years. They came flooding back to him, successively, one after the other. He became nauseous with the memories of the counterfeit Christianity of the Lutheran legacy. But it was all of a piece: Catholic, Orthodox, Lutheran, Protestant; all of it was organized leniency that had precious little to do with the standard and person of Christ.

"I seem to remember I know you," whispered Soren. "You are a coward," he breathed with a far gentler tone than generally accompanies such a statement. "You could not bring yourself to take the final step away from Mother Church in order to preserve your soul. The fight for authentic faith was not palatable to you."

"Soren, it was necessary for me to be at peace with myself. A tenuous peace though it was. But the most disadvantageous peace is better than the most just war. Some say I should have left the institutional church rather than put up with it. I put up with the church in the hope that one day it would become better, just as it was constrained to put up with me in the hope that I would one day become better."

"You defended your sect after having sent others, like Luther, on the path to changing it."

Erasmus intoned curiously, "Sect? There is nothing I congratulate myself on more heartily than on never having joined a sect. I was wed to the church, not Franciscans, nor Dominicans, nor Benedictines, nor any other order."

"To wed yourself to the institution was your sect. Your order was Mother Church. Your god was Holy See. Yet I say to defend something is always to discredit it. Let a man have a warehouse full of gold, let him be willing to give away a coin to every one of the poor—but let him also be stupid enough to begin this charitable undertaking of his with a defense in which he offers three good reasons for doing so. Soon people will find it doubtful whether indeed he is doing something good. The same for Christianity. The person who defends that has never believed in it. If he does believe, then the enthusiasm of faith is not a defense! No, it is the assault and the victory. That's all a believer is: a victor." Soren took a deep breath for the final onslaught. "Indeed, he who first invented the notion of defending Christianity is de facto Judas No. 2. He also betrays with a kiss, only his treachery is that of stupidity!"

Soren's speech crescendoed with an emphatic chant. The demons had been exorcised, once again. His tepid peace was settling in, once again. Erasmus allowed for the pause. He was stung by the insinuation. He knew his courage was of a different kind than Luther's and worlds removed from Kierkegaard's. And yet he would ever have his doubts. After all, now he knew beyond a doubt that no institution endured. No matter how much it progressed, no matter how much it improved. Institutions and organizations were flawed constructs and could never outlive their imperfections. He knew this now. The messiness of organic perfection was still such a mystery, though he knew it was real. Yes, his doubts would persist.

After a few moments, as the two almost imperceptibly increased their walking pace, Erasmus asked, "What do you gain from such hard work?"

The confused look on Soren's face prompted Erasmus to explain. "You beat your head against the wall. For what? What purpose? What benefit? What gain?" He took a breath and continued, "I myself told popes and cardinals to look at the Apostles, and make themselves more like them. And did they? Rarely. Perhaps never. Did I continue to highlight their folly and call them to account? No. Why toil needlessly? Why work to no avail? Why do the same thing over and over expecting a different outcome?"

As the men walked on, time stood still. The midnight hour had drawn on and on. The moon had paused her heavenly course. This clear midwinter night chilled all but the minds of two great thinkers.

At last, Soren began slowly, methodically (a perfect antiphon to the tempo of his walking): "I will attempt to communicate something that thought cannot think." He glanced briefly up through the tangled winter canopy. The moon flashed and danced in a flicker of unthinkable thought. "The gain, or benefit, from my work is precisely that I do not care for anything. I do not care to ride a horse, for the exercise is too violent. I do not care to walk, walking is too strenuous."

"But you are walking now," Erasmus interrupted.

"Ah yes, Socrates understood himself, and thus he thought everyone must understand himself. But one who gives someone not only a thought, but also the condition for understanding the thought, is almost more than a self. I am creating the conditions."

"I see. Apologies for my premature objection. Please continue."

And so Soren did. "I do not care to lie down, for I should have to remain lying, and I do not care to do that, or I should have to get up again, and I do not care to do that either. *Summa summarum*: I do not care at all. Therefore, to work is to look for possibility. To work is to be content with what is while still carrying a passionate sense of the potential. The tension between this *now*, and what *might be*, produces a lasting gain. Whether such benefit is earned or given I'm not sure. Perhaps both."

Erasmus considered Soren's unique response to his questioning. There was no clarity here. There indeed seemed to be something that cannot be thought behind these words. These words, which were an accumulation of apparent nothingness. Yet, there was something compelling behind them.

"Is this paradox?" asked Erasmus.

"Perhaps the absurd is all that can be believed. After all, my Catholic Dutch friend from the fifteenth century, you and I are walking in a Danish wood at midnight."

Erasmus looked ahead. The trees were thinning. They were approaching the far edge of the forest. The walk would soon be over. Rather than attempt any clarification, rather than try to delineate the mystery (which is what he had always done), he allowed himself to imagine that he did not know where this path led.

"The one devoted to the pursuit of wisdom is unlucky in so much; maybe everything," Erasmus said. "Your work, your toil, your hardship is not about some hope for reward, Soren. I can't say I fully see that yet. But I'm beginning to discern a different spectrum of light. Your passion for that sense of potential is compelling."

"Passion and reason are ever my struggling companions," Soren replied.

"How much more passion than reason are we composed of? Some might say scarce half an ounce to a pound. Your words come alive precisely because they rise from the heart."

The two men reached the edge of the wood.

"Here I shall leave you and return from where I came," said Soren. He tipped his head and offered a hand of friendship. "I thank you for the walk. I thank you more for the questions."

Erasmus shook Soren's hand, that faint smile forming in the corner of his mouth once again. He said, "My friend, the existential paradox does not end tonight. If you would accompany me further you might experience fresh mysteries."

"I've never walked this direction beyond the wood. This is the outer limit of Copenhagen. I have at times been considered insane. I myself would be insane if I were to go further."

"I doubt if a single individual could be found from the whole of humanity free from some form of insanity. The only difference is one of degree."

Soren felt the leap stirring up within him. "What is the connection between my inability to raise significant objection and my obligation to believe there is something beyond which my reason rebels?"

"That connection might be considered your new work, or your continued toil."

Soren inhaled deeply and fixed his resolve. He took two deliberate steps beyond the wood. Then, turning to Erasmus, he asked, "Shall we?"

4

Nietzsche and Chesterton in the Pub

Is there anything new under the sun?

—QOHELETH

(*At rise, we see CHESTERTON and NIETZSCHE seated around a small table, just left of center stage. CHESTERTON has an empty pint glass in front of him and drinks from another, half empty. To the right is a long bar, containing several beer taps and pumps. A BAR-TENDER stands behind the now vacant bar, reading a book, tending to something, once or twice exiting behind the bar, then returning and occasionally tending to something else throughout the scene.*)

CHESTERTON (*slamming his hand on the table*)

Damn it all, Friedrich! The riddles of God are always more satisfying than our human solutions.

NIETZSCHE

You state that as a matter of fact, Gilbert. But there are no facts, only interpretations. And this is not a statement of fact, merely an observation. And a good one.

CHESTERTON

The word "good" has many meanings. For example, if a man were to shoot his grandmother at a range of five hundred yards, I should call him a good shot, but not necessarily a good man.

NIETZSCHE

I was being supplementary, not contradictory. We often contradict an opinion for no other reason than that we do not like the tone in which it is expressed.

CHESTERTON

Fine, yes. A tremendous insight. But we must have our opinions and have them with conviction, mustn't we? There's nothing I find more flaccidly spineless than impartiality. Impartiality is a pompous name for indifference, which is an elegant name for ignorance.

NIETZSCHE

Yet, is not our freedom an indifference?

CHESTERTON

How so, my good friend?

NIETZSCHE

Freedom is essentially to grow more indifferent to hardship, to severity, to privation, and even to life itself.

CHESTERTON

Hmm . . . Ha . . . Ahem.
> (*He pauses to reflect, then*)
Possibly. Ancient notion. Perhaps an ancient fable. And there is truth in every ancient fable. For example, consider the ancient

symbol of freedom. Now, owls and bats may wander where they will in darkness, and for them as for the skeptics the universe may have no center; kites and vultures may linger as they like over carrion, and for them as for the plutocrats existence may have no origin and no end. But it was far back in the land of legends, where instincts find their true images, that the cry went forth that freedom is an eagle, whose glory is gazing at the sun.

NIETZSCHE (*with a smirk*)

Then our notion of freedom is not new, not even recent, but has been from of old?

CHESTERTON

Possibly older than we could dare to imagine.

NIETZSCHE

I doubt I believe in newness at all, in fact.

CHESTERTON

Come now, you have no business to be an unbeliever! You ought to stand for all the things stupid people call superstitions. Indeed, don't you think there's a lot in those old wives' tales about luck and charms and so on, silver bullets included?

NIETZSCHE

Well, in that light my belief, or absence of belief, is not a factor.

CHESTERTON

Nonsense! It's your business to believe things. You yourself have said that "to be a devotee of truth, one must always inquire."

NIETZSCHE

That applies to tangible things.

CHESTERTON

And the divine is not tangible, I suppose?

NIETZSCHE

Why must belief always be reduced to the sphere of divinity?

CHESTERTON (*ignoring him*)

Oh, atheism is, I suppose, the supreme example of a simple faith.

(*NIETZSCHE, uncharacteristically, laughs a non-caustic laugh.*)

CHESTERTON

Go ahead, say it, friend.

NIETZSCHE (*still chuckling*)

I don't want to grant you the satisfaction!

(*NIETZSCHE calmly returns to his melancholy self, while CHES-TERTON drinks his beer.*)

NIETZSCHE

Barkeep, a tankard if you please. A lager. German.

(*The BARTENDER pours and brings the beer to the table.*)

BARTENDER

Here you are, Mr. Nietzsche.

(*The BARTENDER exits behind the bar for a time. NIETZSCHE sips his beer, wipes his mustache with the back of his sleeve.*)

NIETZSCHE

Well, he is, you know.

CHESTERTON

What? Who?

NIETZSCHE

God. He is dead. And we—

CHESTERTON

Aha! And there you have it. The cause which is blocking all progress today is the subtle skepticism which whispers in a million ears that things are not good enough to be worth improving. Pessimism is now patently, as it always was essentially, more commonplace than piety. Of course, if there was not God there would be no atheist. And indeed it—

NIETZSCHE

Do let me finish, Gilbert. You never let me finish. You always take that isolated statement as your touchstone and jump into the fathomless abyss dragging the whole of civilization with you.

CHESTERTON

Very well then, old friend.

NIETZSCHE

As I was saying, God is dead, and we have killed him. How shall we comfort ourselves, the murderers of all murderers? What was holiest and mightiest of all that the world has yet owned has bled to death under our knives. Who will wipe this blood off us? What water is there for us to clean ourselves? What festivals of atonement, what sacred games shall we have to invent? Is not the greatness of this deed too great for us? Must we ourselves not become gods simply to appear worthy of it?

CHESTERTON

Hmm. I see. So not the genesis of divinity nor the murder of the divine is new at all, is it?

NIETZSCHE

Indeed. Therefore, I don't believe in newness. And what I mean about belief in newness is this: consider the modern scientific counterpart to belief in God, which is the belief in the universe as an organism. This disgusts me. This is to make what is quite rare and extremely derivative, the organic, which we perceive only on the surface of the earth, into something essential, universal, and eternal! This is still an anthropomorphizing of nature! It is not new in the least.

CHESTERTON

And your conclusion is that nothing can be made new?

NIETZSCHE

What if the newness is in our interpretation, rather than the objects themselves. After all there are no—

CHESTERTON

No facts, only interpretations. So you've said.

NIETZSCHE

Indeed.

CHESTERTON

Quite. Quite. Or . . . rather . . . palpable balderdash!

NIETZSCHE

Not at all. We believe that we know something about the things themselves when we speak of trees, colors, snow, and flowers. And yet we possess nothing but metaphors for things—metaphors which correspond in no way to the original entities.

CHESTERTON

Oh come, Friedrich. You are flitting with concepts and forms as if you're playing at pick-up sticks.

NIETZSCHE

Concepts and forms? We only obtain any concept, as we do any form, by overlooking what is individual and actual; whereas nature is acquainted with no forms and no concepts, and likewise with no species, but only with an X which remains inaccessible and undefinable for us.

CHESTERTON

Truth then is a moving target?

NIETZSCHE

Almost. It is a movable host of metaphors, metonymies, and anthropomorphisms: in short, a sum of human relations which have been poetically and rhetorically intensified, transferred, and embellished, and which, after long usage, seem to a people to be fixed, canonical, and binding.

(*CHESTERTON slams his hand on the table. With the other hand, he drains his pint, then holds the empty glass aloft.*)

CHESTERTON

Another English ale, old chap.

(*The BARTENDER pours another beer and brings it to the table, clearing the empty glasses and tidying up as he goes.*)

NIETZSCHE

That makes three, Gilbert.

CHESTERTON

Ha! One pint is enough, two pints is one too many, three pints isn't half enough!

NIETZSCHE

You should really try our German lager: *helles.*

CHESTERTON

Is it a metaphorical or actual beer? You see, I prefer my beer to resemble my existence: both bearing a moral reality.

NIETZSCHE

Our lager is the distillation of moral reality in action. For everything which distinguishes man from the animals depends upon this ability to volatilize perceptual metaphors in a schema, and thus to distill an image into a concept. We have taken the image of light, the *helles*, and distilled it into a pint. This is truth.

CHESTERTON

Not only the over-man, but now the over-beer, I see!

NIETZSCHE

Anything less would be a laughingstock and a painful embarrassment.

CHESTERTON

Do you honestly think that, Friedrich? It seems all your "over" and "super" descriptors are the result of timid thinking.

NIETZSCHE

I am not timid when it comes to beer. And, since German beer is the pinnacle of brewing achievement, it goes further to substantiate my insistence that nothing is new.

CHESTERTON

Well why not say "a purer beer" or "a happier beer"? Such statements as these would be truly alarming and remarkable ideas. They say something. To say "over" or "upper" or "super" is just a physical metaphor derived from acrobats, or maybe climbers.

NIETZSCHE

We possess nothing but metaphors which—

CHESTERTON

Which correspond in no way to the original entities. Yes, you've said that, too. Being a bit circular, aren't we? Look, take your German beer. Let's consider it the supreme beer. The over-beer, the super-beer. A suggestion I heartily disagree with, of course, but for the sake of discussion I concede you this point to throttle headfirst toward another. Here it is: how do we come to have a beer which is beyond all other beer? If humanity has been so magnanimous as to select it, how did we manage to do so? Was it because of the beer's qualities? Is the beer the zenith of malt perfection? Are the hops perfectly understated? Or maybe your *helles* contains more just, braver, and merciful notes than our sub-standard top-fermented cask English ales?

NIETZSCHE

Gilbert, you are talking about people.

CHESTERTON

Beer, my friend. Only beer. Ever beer. But, if I may be permitted to extend the brewing metaphor further, you have mocked the casks of the forgotten past, only to discover some new beer in an un-imaginable—and apparently German—future!

NIETZSCHE

The metaphor is strained, my friend. But I see you are criticiz-ing not just the higher beer, but the higher self. And why so? We should not fear our higher self just because when it speaks, it speaks demandingly.

CHESTERTON

But you cannot discount the old and claim there is no new while simultaneously embracing something new, however impossible it seems. You have laid all blame on ideals, and yet you have set up the most impossible of all ideals: the ideal of a new creature who is self-made.

NIETZSCHE

To call it new is merely a matter of grammar; slight of hand.

CHESTERTON

But it is your hand, dear fellow. Not mine!

NIETZSCHE

Very well, I concede that I am after something new. But, as of yet, there has been nothing new. Therefore, from the dawn of history until now, there is nothing new. This new thing, this superhuman is still in our future. We long for it without yet knowing it, without seeing it. And we press forward with our world of metaphors which continually manifests an ardent desire to refashion reality. Which presents itself to waking humanity, so that it will be as colorful, irregular, lacking in results and coherence, charming, and eternally new as the world of dreams.

CHESTERTON

See, this is our greatest point of distance, Friedrich. It is not my embrace of an eternal God versus your rejection of divinity. It is in where we place the new thing on the historical spectrum. You are looking ever forward. I say the new has dawned in the ancient past. You do not see things as they really are. If you did, you would fall on your knees before them. It is not seeing things as they are to imagine a demigod of infinite mental clarity, who may or may not appear in the latter days of the earth, and then to see all the rest of us through history as idiots. When we really see others as they are, we do not criticize, but worship; and very rightly. For a monster with mysterious eyes and miraculous thumbs, with strange dreams in his skull, and a queer tenderness for this place or that baby, is truly a wonderful and unnerving matter. It is only the quite arbitrary and priggish habit of comparison with something else which makes it possible to be at our ease in front of him. A sentiment of superiority keeps us cool and practical; the mere facts would make our knees knock under with fear. It is the fact that every instant of conscious life is an unimaginable prodigy. It is the fact that every face in the street has the incredible unexpectedness of a fairy tale! If you saw things as they are, you would realize that the new thing you seek is as old and ancient as humanity. When we dawned into the universe, the final new thing—and the most unfathomable— was ushered into experience.

NIETZSCHE

To really see things, as you suggest, then is to see reality in reverse.

CHESTERTON

Perhaps we must be reminded of going back to the old even to find the new.

NIETZSCHE

What then do we do with your Christ? If the new thing is as ancient as the dawning of humanity, how can there be a claim to a new thing in him?

CHESTERTON

Ah! Now there is a question, my friend. The everlasting man, this Christ, showed us what the new fully looked like. We could not call the ancient new without seeing it completely realized in him. Therefore, he shows us not something new, but all things being made new in light of the ancient purpose.

(*NIETZSCHE muses on this recent volley from CHESTERTON. As he does so he sips his tankard. Meanwhile, CHESTERTON intermittently chuckles as he quaffs his ale.*)

NIETZSCHE

I suppose in the span of your drinking three more of your English pints, you'll soon be telling me that somehow this newness is even incarnated in our own spirits, and our natures are inclusive of this power but with no will toward it.

(*CHESTERTON lets out a full-throated and generous laugh. There is no malice in it. No retribution. No superiority.*)

CHESTERTON

Friedrich, my old friend. Your ability to crystalize truth never ceases to amaze me. Here's to the old that is new.

(*CHESTERTON holds forth his pint glass for a toast. NIETZSCHE pauses, smiles, then clinks his tankard to CHESTERTON's glass in mutual appreciation. They drink their beers in silence.*)

LIGHTS OUT.

5

Virginia and Albert at Sea

What advantage have the wise over fools?

—QOHELETH

14 June 1938

IT WAS A TRANSATLANTIC journey of a mere four days. Time for
me to read, and write, and fill my lungs with the fresh winds of the
sea. The potential of moving a bit out of this perpetual shadow was
on the horizon. Unremarkable really, except for last night; our final
night at sea. That's when he said to me, "We must color the void."

I did not know Albert before yesterday eve. But we found
ourselves seated at dinner simultaneously. And as the dining sa-
loon was crowded, we found ourselves seated opposite each other.
Underneath the oaken splendor of the chateaux dome, I found
myself engaged in a dinner conversation with the man who I now
know as a paradox of the absurd.

This young man, scarcely a quarter of a century behind him,
made quite the impression on me. Here I was, an aging woman,

merely taking a summer trip to lighten my horizons in the New World; and now I'm contemplating multiple new worlds. The strange thing about life is that, though the nature of it must have been apparent to everyone for hundreds of years, no one has left any adequate account of it. The streets of London have their map; the sea routes from England to America have their nautical charts; but our passions are uncharted. Who are you going to meet if you turn this corner?

The wineglasses had been filled yellow and crimson, had been emptied, had been filled again when he said it: "We must color the void." It was that paradoxical turn of phrase that sent me reeling. He had been waxing paradoxical all evening. I should have been prepared for it; staunched against the next rush of absurdity. But yet, this short declaration that what was empty of all light, all vividness, could be recreated anew—such notions will ever catch me short of breath.

He had paved the way for this remarkable statement with a multitude of aphorisms, the summation of each particular compounded upon the former in a dizzying array of slant wisdom. That is to say, he spoke just to the side of wise. Each remark held a profound kernel of truth which was modified by its antecedents with ideas that presented themselves at cross-purposes with the whole. Or were the ancillary thoughts the true mark? Was the slant because I was looking head-on at what was meant to be viewed sideways? I cannot tell. I could not tell. Albert pontificated about an existence that is both illusory and eternal; the act of creation that is not true creation without a secret to unfold; a world that is only clear if no art exists. Somewhere hovering near the borders of these sagacious felicities was the clarion light of wisdom. But its dawn was ever moved just behind the horizon with each new turn of phrase, each addendum of verbosity, each litany of words. Light here does require a shadow there.

Midway through the pheasant course—many and various, with all their retinue of sauces and salads, the sharp and the sweet, each in its order, and their potatoes, thin as coins but not so hard, for one cannot think well if one has not dined well—he'd said, "A profound thought is in a constant state of becoming; it adopts the experience of a life and assumes its shape."

"That itself is a curious thought, Mr. Camus," I replied. He is adding too much to the simplicity of the idea, I thought. It is as if his own thought plunged into a sea of words and came up dripping.

He went on. "Consider how thoughts complement one another, Mrs. Woolf. They correct or overtake one another, contradict one another, too. To be true, a succession of thoughts can be but a series of approximations of the same thought. But it is possible to conceive of another type of thought which communicates by juxtaposition. The words of that thought may seem to be devoid of interrelations, and to a certain degree, they are contradictory. But viewed all together, they resume their natural grouping as one thought."

Ah, this is absurdism, I thought.

No sooner had this thought—whether complemented, juxtaposed, or still in a state of becoming, I could not tell—been introduced into the pause between us than the silent servingman, attending to our table as if we were parishioners, this hall the church, and he the beadle, set before us, wreathed in napkins, a confection which rose all sugar from the waves. Whether the sweet rush flushed my cheeks or no, I felt piqued when Albert spoke of the ironic philosophies that produce passionate works; how Oedipus teaches us that all has not been exhausted; why there are always apologetics for simple lack of courage. And as the dessert was laid before us—which to call it pudding and so relate it to rice and tapioca would be an insult—Albert went on unfolding conundrums. He insisted that absolute freedom mocks at justice, absolute justice denies freedom; thus to be fruitful, the two ideas must find their limits in each other.

Just so, we finished our courses, sipping the wine again, and thus by degrees was lit, halfway down the spine, which is the seat of the soul, not that hard little electric light which we call brilliance, as it pops in and out upon our lips, but the more profound, subtle and subterranean glow which is the rich yellow flame of rational intercourse. No need to hurry. No need to sparkle. No need to be anybody but oneself.

And we talked. Or rather mostly he talked. I marveled. It was not the profundity of his talk that I marveled at. I have had the pleasure of being the intended audience of wiser men, and much wiser women. Rather, it was the perhaps unintended result of such paradoxical absurdism to make wisdom a play thing. Wisdom was somehow becoming secondary or even tertiary to our state of being. I was astonished at the mere volume of language. I joined with the prince of Denmark: "Words, words, words!" And such words, too. Words. You can, of course, catch them and sort them and place them in alphabetical order in dictionaries. But words do not live in dictionaries, they live in the mind. If you want proof of this, consider how often in moments of emotion when we most need words we find none. Yet there is the dictionary; there at our disposal are some half-a-million words all in alphabetical order. But can we use them? No. And yet, look once more at the diction-ary. There beyond a doubt lie plays more splendid than *Anthony and Cleopatra*, poems lovelier than the "Ode to a Nightingale," novels beside which *Pride and Prejudice* or *David Copperfield* are the crude bunglings of amateurs. It is only a question of finding the right words and putting them in the right order. But we cannot do it because they do not live in dictionaries, they live in the mind.

At any rate, my mind was weaving through the assaulting array of Albert's words. Not that he meant them to assault; there was no violence in his intent; likely no notion that his paradoxes and absurdities were a chaotic interplay of question without re-sponse. Life is, after all, not a series of gig lamps symmetrically arranged; life is a luminous halo, a semi-transparent envelope surrounding us from the beginning of consciousness to the end. And midway through the second after-dinner cordial—or was it the third? fourth?—this young man's unintended assault on my conscious was dizzying. No one can escape the power of language, I suppose, let alone those of English birth brought up from child-hood, as I had been, to frolic now in the Saxon plainness, now in the Latin splendor of the tongue, and stored with memories of old poets delighting in an infinity of vocabularies. Somewhere between the exclamation that art is the activity which exalts and denies simultaneously—"After all, as Nietzsche has said," quoth he, "no artist tolerates reality"—and asserting the rebellious contradiction that man rejects the world without accepting the necessity for escaping it, Albert acquiesced to the need for a study of Shakespeare's sonnets as a preliminary to undertaking any number of biographies. And then with a perfectly frivolous jest, he evolved a theory that Anne Hathaway had a way, among other things, of writing Shakespeare's sonnets; the idea struck out to enliven a party of professors—who could not but hear the suggestion made at such a volume—which began to debate Albert's joke in earnest. He took brief notice of this and let them continue their path, for his jokes were, as he said, at least as good as other people's facts.

And then he returned to the mysterious clarity of the artist. It was the artist who reconstructed the world to her own reality. And I noticed that he intentionally used the feminine pronoun in deference to my presence. How sad, he thought himself evolved because of it; though he clearly did not object to my own thinking; thinking however and about whatever I wished. Usually nobody objects to a woman thinking unless she is thinking of something other than man. But to return to the artist, he said that the wisdom is in seeing ourselves like a work of art. With this, he gestured to the canvas hanging over my right shoulder. I gazed up at it and considered how the mind of an artist, in order to achieve the prodigious effort of freeing whole and entire the work that is in him, must be incandescent. There must be no obstacle in the artistic mind, no foreign matter unconsumed. How exhausting. Surely the artist must rest for a moment. And, resting, Albert and I looked from each other vaguely to the canvas again. And there it was, the old question which transversed the sky of the soul perpetually, the vast, the general question which was apt to particularize itself at such moments as these: what is the meaning of life?

That was all—a simple question; one that tended to close in on one with years. The great revelation had never come to me; not entirely. This young man seemed to have already given up the question. No, the great revelation perhaps never did come. Instead, there were little daily miracles, illuminations, matches struck unexpectedly in the dark; here was one. This, that, and the other. Every moment of idleness a new match struck. It is in our idleness that the submerged truth sometimes comes to the top.

We have looked at the meaning of life from the grand perspective, on the scale of universes. But when you consider things like the stars, our affairs don't seem to matter very much, do they? Yet, in the minutiae of particularity is where meaning is most prevalent. And perhaps therein was the key to finding the wisdom just to the side of Albert's words. One must follow hints, not exactly what is said, nor yet entirely what is done. This was true of his work of redefining and recapitulating the meaning of sense, as in when he spoke of nihilism, which he said is not to believe in nothing, but to not believe in what actually is.

The void. The void actually is. The void is not nothing. It is there. And here. And it exists perpetually as a void. What to do then?

"We must color the void," he said. "That is the meaning of life."

How exquisitely strange and terrifying it is in those existential moments of transcendence when so much becomes clear and yet inexpressible at the same time. That which is, is far off, and very deep, and hidden. And yet, it can be brought to illumination through colorscape. Like a sculptor with his clay, one can accept that one's creation has no future; it may be destroyed in a day or it may last centuries, neither option having fundamentally more importance than the other. This is difficult wisdom. Perhaps it is absurd. If it is the color beyond the void, if it is a magnification while simultaneously a negation, then it is something other than nothing. No, that's not quite right. It is something more than nothing. No, not exactly that either. Maybe it is something beyond nothing.

To all the new worlds, indeed. And beyond.

Interlude

God the Little Boy

WHAT IS GOD LIKE?

Sometimes I imagine God as a Little Boy.

Each day when the Boy awakens he leaps out of bed with an expectation of newness. All things are new.

Experience is the vehicle of joy.

Yesterday has passed and is forgotten as if flung to the depths of the sea. And anything after today is just that: after today.

This moment, this span of time, is what matters most to the Boy.

God the Boy plunges headlong into the world with unbridled innocence. He laughs with sheer delight at the encounter of new things: an unknown machine, a brand new sound, a joke, a concept never before grasped.

When he goes on an adventure walk to discover the undiscovered, he is giddy with the mere anticipation of it all.

And when his heart is broken, as it regularly is, emotion is not withheld. God the Boy throws his body into the convulsing sobs of disillusionment. He writhes in the pain of a stubbed toe. He screams in anger when disappointment devastates his dreams.

God the Boy's giant emotions stem from his deep love of all people, creatures, and things. He clings to the ones he loves; defends even the inanimate things that have sprung from the recesses of his imagination; lavishes those who honor him with gratitude and undying grace.

6

The First Christian Humanist

Artes humanitatis reddant nos humanos a Deo.

—JUAN LUIS VIVES

HE IS OBVIOUSLY AN existentialist, this Qoheleth of ours. I say obviously because of the persistent questions he poses that are trying to somehow get at what life is all about. Why are we here? What does it all mean? And so forth. There is a certain angst that partially forms the existential foundation of his three most pressing questions:

- What do people gain from all their toil?
- Is there anything new under the sun?
- What advantage have the wise over fools?

And as I've mentioned, all these questions are wrapped up into Qoheleth's investigation that is a quest for the purpose of life.

Now I want to suggest that Qoheleth is also the first Christian humanist. Humanist, because of his concern with the nature of humanity. Christian, because he hints at answers that lead in a direct logically posited line to Christ.

For Qoheleth, humanity is a central concern; so much so, that our brave speaker may be foreshadowing incarnational living. He seems to suggest that as we become more human, we somehow become clearer perfections of what is beyond human, even divine. As such, Qoheleth is unabashedly humanistic. So, too, is Christ's life and focus humanistic. You see, humanism is the very essence of incarnation. God took on the particularity of humanity, he did not do away with humanity. Eternal life may or may not have to do with a length of time; i.e., eternity. But it certainly has to do with quality. Eternity is something of God-quality life in this space and time, in the present moment. It is a continuation of the gift of life right here and now. This is so much a gift, that those who can see the beauty of this gifted life, must get their hands dirty for the sake of others who cannot yet see the beauty. And that's exactly what Qoheleth is doing. He boldly dives headlong into the unbearable process of describing life as it really is. He is brave enough to do what we are rarely brave enough to do. We deceive ourselves into thinking that the more we toil, the harder we work, the more satisfied we will be. We begin to find our identity not only in our work, but ultimately in dominating the other. And who is this other? Everyone. Anyone not us, and, often, anyone not like us. Qoheleth is reminding us that our identity must rather be found in the one who gifts us with this very life and work.

It is in the search and fleshing out of the primary questions he raises that Qoheleth exerts himself as the first Christian humanist. Let's look at the three questions in a way which I hope will evidence some of the humanist strains of Qoheleth's thinking. We'll bring in some partners along the path: themselves existentialist, or humanist, or both, plus a little more.

What's the Point?

The nothingness, the void, the wind, the meaninglessness, the very existence of *hebel* is absurd. Soren Kierkegaard certainly shares in

Qoheleth's recognition of the absurdity of *hebel*: "How empty and meaningless life is."[1] For Kierkegaard, common sense and reason become confines over which one must leap into the even more absurd. In his case, that which is beyond absurd is an embracing of the Christian faith, while simultaneously rejecting the structured system of Christendom. Such a life provides unity for the ethical and aesthetic life, thereby creating coherence for the individual's holistic life. Yet, Kierkegaard notes that this coherency, which does provide gain for the individual, may provide too much meaning. He argues that no part of life ought to have so much meaning that a person cannot forget it at any moment; on the other hand, every single part of life ought to have so much meaning that a person can remember it at any moment. This paradoxical response to Qoheleth's quest for gain, or meaning, certainly seems to be an either/or proposition. Either there is no gain, or there is too much gain. Additionally, in order to realize this gain, the individual must act, must leap, must strive for it.

Turning to Erasmus of Rotterdam, we at first find a recognition and acceptance of toil as something good: "Nothing fine is ever done without struggle."[2] Erasmus was one of the early humanists who wanted something more than mere knowledge: a metaphysics that would reformulate knowledge. For Erasmus, it is the human mind, the capacity for reason, that manifests as the desired good. Though this may lead us into complications in our third considered question, for now let's accept Erasmus' understanding. Though reflection may be hard work, it is the very capacity of the human mind that makes the struggle worthwhile. Erasmus concurs with Qoheleth that nature has created humanity weak and defenseless, but as compensation, we have a mind equipped for knowledge. And the capacity for understanding, if properly implemented and humbly accepted, contains all other possibilities and capacities. Herein lies the concept of giftedness. Gift, not in a superior sense, but as a reality, is embedded at the heart of Qoheleth's

---

1. See Kierkegaard, *Either/Or: A Fragment of Life.*
2. See Erasmus, "Antibarbarians."

quest to discover the gain that comes from toil. Erasmus points us toward the giftedness that constitutes gain.

This idea of gift is tied to the idea of leisure that runs throughout Ecclesiastes. Folks who know very little about Qoheleth can still finish this sentence: "Eat, drink, and be merry . . ." Yep, that's his line. Tomorrow we may die, but the leisure Qoheleth recommends is no mere idleness. Why? Because Qoheleth notes repeatedly that idleness produces no gain. Josef Pieper—a twentieth-century German philosopher heavily influenced by Aquinas—suggests that leisure is not something to be attained through strained effort, nor sacrifice without purpose. Instead, leisure becomes gift. Gift becomes the antithesis of sloth, which is Kierkegaard's despair from weakness. More specifically, it is gift received that is sloth's antithesis. For humanity's happiness and cheerful affirmation of our own natural being results from our "acquiescence in the world and in God—which is to say love."[3] Consequently, leisure becomes the opposite of idleness.

As Qoheleth continues to ask after *yithron*, this everlasting gain, there emerges an awareness that gain must be discovered as something that is granted to those who receive it. It is gifted, much like the capacity of the mind and the potential for leisure. Gain is blessing; it is a superabundance that is discerned by the workers in life who have eyes to see the giving of purpose, even in the midst of strenuous labor, toil, and weariness. How can there be superabundance and blessing in hard work? Qoheleth certainly has observed that blessing does not come from the act of the work itself. This is the perverted mindset that has fed the flawed world he sees. It leads to humanity toiling endlessly in order to find fulfillment and satisfaction, whether through pleasures, knowledge, or any number of efforts that do not in and of themselves yield blessing. Rather, a lasting gain comes through the tension of creaturely response to the creator-God. This that we have allows space for us to provide something that we don't yet have. It gives humanity a chance to go beyond nothingness and create something. This something may be found in Ecclesiastes 3:10: "I have seen the business that God

3. Pieper, *Leisure: The Basis of Culture*, 45.

has given to everyone to be busy with." This phrase carries a suggestion of bowed down activity in response to something greater than that outside one's self. Strains of transcendence are markedly in Qoheleth's mind. It appears that creator and creation must work together in an attitude of cooperation for gain to be realized and received. This is a focus on the human self: humanist. And it is also a focus on cooperation with the divine: Christian.

If you haven't yet read chapter 3 of this book, there you'll find a completely different way of dealing with this first of Qoheleth's three major questions.

What's New?

Now let's take up the second of Qoheleth's three major questions, which has to do with the idea of newness: "Is there a thing of which it is said, 'See, this is new'?" (1:10). The question is inherent at many points throughout the book. This question persists because Qoheleth has seen many human activities and strivings that purport to bring meaning to life, but each one fails in its intent. It all has been tried before, and nothing succeeds in its intended quest. At least, the success doesn't seem to have much to do with our understanding of success. If there is newness, it sure doesn't look new at all.

The oft-misinterpreted Friedrich Nietzsche also endeavored to discover something new, though he might have considered it ancient, dormant, waiting just beneath the surface to be discovered. His struggle was with developing a positive and affirming philosophy regarding meaning. The result of his efforts is distilled in his seminal phrase, "All meaning is will to power."[4] Though a new turn of phrase, this was no new concept. Placing all emphasis on the individual, the Superman, or Overman, as the ground and intent of all meaning does little to satisfy Qoheleth's quest for newness. Nietzsche's "new" concept was in fact a reworking and reinterpretation of much of Arthur Schopenhauer's own points, though Nietzsche paints it as a rebuttal of Schopenhauer. Nothing new under the sun, indeed.

4. See Nietzsche, *Will to Power*.

A Christian humanist quest for the new fully recognizes the foundation of the old which it builds upon. Rejecting or denying even the existence for the former is not an option. It is in this same vein that the Hebrew prophets built upon the narratives of their ancestors. In building on that narrative, they also reinterpreted it, contextualized it to their given circumstance and society, and re-narrated that which was old in a new way. They attempted to translate the universality of the human condition into the particularity of their own stories. Leonardo Bruni, the early Renaissance proponent of the *studia humanitatis*—a fifteenth-century course of classical studies including rhetoric, philosophy, ethics, poetry, grammar, and mathematics—recognized the teachings that went before him. In working out his ethics of human nature from the milieu of literature, he first turned to the Greeks and Romans to consider "whether human felicity consists in pleasure and the absence of pain, as Epicurus would have it, or in moral worth, as Zeno believed, or in the exercise of virtue, which was Aristotle's view."[5] Bruni then could synthesize a particular view, only informed by the opinions of the past, for his specific context.

Many humane thinkers throughout history have recognized that study of the ancients, immersion in that which is classical, is a humanistic endeavor, since knowledge of the old makes us human. It is only by turning halfway around, where one can be firmly rooted in the past and in the present simultaneously, that anything new can be realized. Re-traditioning is only possible when tradition is fully examined. Nor can a robust and wizened view of human nature exist independent of the past. This is why Giambattista Vico—one of the several Italian interdisciplinary thinkers from the last several centuries—shows us that to study the past is to find a way forward from the present into the future: "Indeed, if we ourselves contemplate our own corrupted human nature we will discover that it not only points out to us [that] which we must cultivate but will also clearly disclose the order and path by which we shall approach [it]."[6] The old ways manifest themselves as new

5. See Bruni, "On The Study of Literature."
6. See Vico, "On the Proper Order."

to us, and to Qoheleth, because we have forgotten them and need to be reminded of their truth. Perhaps we need more folks like G. K. Chesterton to remind us about going back to the old even to find the new.[7]

In chapter 4 of this book, you can experience a short dramatic scene that suggests a unique perspective on the second question. Add one part Nietzsche, one part Chesterton, and an ample supply of beer, then see what happens.

Why Wisdom?

Our third question seeks a *telos*—that is, a point, a purpose, or an end—to wisdom: "What happens to the fool will happen to me also; why then have I been so very wise?" (Eccl 2:15). Qoheleth asks this another way elsewhere: "For what advantage have the wise over fools?" (6:8). Qoheleth sees wisdom primarily used by his society as a tool to obtain something else. Here is where, though firmly rooted in the wisdom tradition, he criticizes it. For Qoheleth, even turning to the sapiential framework and following it by rote is in the end *hebel*. What's more, to toil with wisdom and knowledge is pointless if the reward of the toil goes to the one who does not seek the wisdom.

Qoheleth specifically confronts the structure of traditional wisdom and sapiential thought in Hebrew Scripture. It is clear that Qoheleth is at home in the world of Hebrew wisdom, and yet wisdom is on trial. He lays out an observatory case against conventional wisdom from within the school of wisdom with, at times, a satirical tone. Here is not only an implosion of wisdom, but a purifying of the tradition itself. Qoheleth struggles with the so-called traditions of his people, intently observing the ramifications of proverbial understanding, and recognizing the inherent problems with strains of traditional wisdom thought. What his community has lauded as tradition may be nothing more than traditionalism. In other words, the way of the wise is precisely as it is because that's

7. See Chesterton, "New Jerusalem."

the way his community had done it for centuries, not because the way honors the spirit of wisdom. Amazingly, Qoheleth devastatingly makes this investigation not as a rebel, not as an outsider, but from within the world of wisdom. Yet, in this world of wisdom, Qoheleth finds himself to be a stranger, and his implicit call is that those who would be truly wise will also find themselves strangers. Qoheleth would concur with Hugh of Saint Victor: "All the world is foreign soil to those who philosophize."[8] Qoheleth would likely consider himself orthodox, but this book is composed so fully of unorthodox speeches. This is the genius of Qoheleth—and reflects the humble act of faith from our spiritual ancestors who canonized this book—wherein he is not glibly espousing orthodox teaching, as do Job's three so-called friends. Rather he reimagines the intent of orthodox wisdom, connecting it to the life of the God who is creator, in a blaze of brave honesty.

What then is the purpose of wisdom? Several centuries after Kierkegaard, an absurdist existentialist—though he rejected that classification—tried to synthesize the trajectory of the human condition: "I rebel, therefore we exist."[9] Albert Camus would concur with Qoheleth that seeking wisdom is futile, and then would have us revolt against all that comes before in order to gain one human truth—namely, defiance. This defiance is also blasted in the face of death in order to affirm life. There is an absolutism in this absurdist view that would not be acclimated to Qoheleth's lens. If Qoheleth rejects the past, then how can it be re-traditioned into newness? If Qoheleth expends time and energy on defying death, then how can gain be received in the present moment? Of any number of possible responses to Qoheleth's question, Camus gives at once the easiest and yet the most unattainable. One can picture Qoheleth hearing Camus' response, staring blankly at the man, shrugging his shoulders, and continuing to question as if uninterrupted. It is as if the answer supplied was for a different question entirely. Or maybe Qoheleth would say, "All this I have tested by wisdom, but it was far from me. That which is, is far off, and deep, very deep;

8. Victore, *Didascalicon.*

9. See Camus, *Rebel.*

who can find it out?" (7:23–24). And then he would still continue the search.

It seems the locus of the question of wisdom is placed in the person of the divine. John Henry Newman rejects any utilitarian intent in pursuing wisdom (note that Newman is using "knowledge" here, meaning the same as Qoheleth's "wisdom"): "Knowledge is capable of being its own end. Such is the constitution of the human mind, that any kind of knowledge, if it be really such, is its own reward."[10] There is no other use for wisdom apart from the thing itself. But how can this be so? Yet another paradox. Qoheleth and all those we've encountered in various other places in this book give us questions, question us, lead us to discover our own questions, beg more questions, and never seem to give us answers. So maybe the question "How can this be so?" is its own answer.

In chapter 5 of this book, you will find yet another way to consider how all this about wisdom can be so.

Qoheleth's eyes have been opened to all the *hebel* he has discovered. He has a litany of questions. And so might we. Yet in the midst of this world of *hebel*, Qoheleth recognizes that God gifts us with joy in life's toil, evident in gain received as gift. And so might we. Qoheleth perceives that newness can be discovered by looking back and reimagining the old. And so might we. Qoheleth dares to suggest that the point of wisdom is in its pursuit. And so might we.

10. See John Henry Newman, "The Idea of a University."

7

Pursuing What's Hidden

Gradually as the sky whitened a dark line lay on the horizon dividing the sea from the sky and the grey cloth became barred with thick strokes moving, one after another, beneath the surface, following each other, pursuing each other, perpetually.

—VIRGINIA WOOLF

IN THIS CHAPTER I want to try something a bit daring. I will likely fail, and here it will remain in print for others to be amused by my failure. But I'm good at failure, and, frankly, I tend to learn a lot from it. Consider this an homage to Qoheleth, who tried to translate the incongruities, traditions, and absurdities he observed into something meaningful. And here's what I'm going to attempt: I will be translating one passage from the words of Qoheleth, then trying to explain some of the thinking going on behind the words and my translation of them. I'm doing this in the hope that you will be engaged enough, excited enough, upset enough, curious enough, offended enough, inspired enough to pursue what's hidden on your own. That is, after all, at the essence of what Qoheleth seems to conclude is the meaning of life. The meaning is in the pursuit.

Here we go.

The passage is from Ecclesiastes 3:9–15. It comes after the only passage from Ecclesiastes used in any of the church calendar lectionaries. The first eight verses of chapter three are so well-known that they have inspired songs, poetry, and paintings many times over: "A time to live, a time to die," and so on. What I will focus on comes after the passage that gets all the credit. It is the something beyond the familiar.

First, let me give you a standard translation of this passage from the NRSV:

> What gain have the workers from their toil? I have seen the business that God has given to everyone to be busy with. He has made everything suitable for its time; moreover, he has put a sense of past and future into their minds, yet they cannot find out what God has done from the beginning to the end. I know that there is nothing better for them than to be happy and enjoy themselves as long as they live; moreover, it is God's gift that all should eat and drink and take pleasure in all their toil. I know that whatever God does endures forever; nothing can be added to it, nor anything taken from it; God has done this, so that all should stand in awe before him. That which is, already has been; that which is to be, already is; and God seeks out what has gone by.

Now, here is my translation:

> What excellence do the workers realize from their hard work? I have examined the task God has given to everyone which creates space for response. God does all things beautifully in their time; likewise, God has put a sense of transcendence into humans' inner beings, yet they cannot grasp the beginning nor end of what God does. I realized the best thing for them is to receive happiness and delight in life as long as they live, because it is God's gift that all humanity should eat and drink and discover goodness in their work. I conclude that all of God's actions will

continue forever: there is nothing to add nor subtract—
they are complete. God does this to invite all into worship.
Everything that is, has been; everything that will be, is; and
God invites humanity to pursue what is hidden.

Exegesis

Here is Qoheleth once again touching on that pervasive inquiry:
gain that may or may not come as a result of hard work. *Yithron*—
"gain" or "excellence"—rests at the heart of the question. Gain is
not something that can be attained or earned. As Qoheleth continues to ask after this gain throughout Ecclesiastes, there emerges
an awareness that gain must be discovered as something that is
granted to those who receive it; it is a gift. *Yithron* is more a blessing than that which can count as gain or profit; it is an excellence
that is discerned by the workers in life who have eyes to see the
giving of purpose, even in the midst of strenuous labor, toil, and
weariness. Why excellence? Because we cannot give a gift to ourselves. Oh, we can try. But there is something far more excellent in
the crude picture my seven-year-old daughter draws and hands to
me with a "This is for you, Daddy" than I could ever generate from
anything I may purchase for myself.

And yet, how can there be excellence in toil; where is the
blessing in hard work? Qoheleth certainly has observed that
blessing does not come from the act of the work itself. This is the
perverted mindset that has fed the flawed world he sees. It leads
to humanity toiling endlessly in order to find fulfillment and satisfaction; whether through pleasures, virtues, or any number of
efforts that do not in and of themselves yield blessing. Rather, the
excellence comes through the tension of creaturely response to
the creator-God. *Nathan*—"gives" or "creates space"—carries the
double meaning of giving and opening up. This task that God has
given is also opening up space for something from humanity. This
something may be found in the phrase "to be busy with" (NRSV).
The root is *'anah*, which carries a suggestion of "bowed down activity" in response to something greater than that outside oneself.

Strains of transcendence are markedly in Qoheleth's mind as the next couple of verses will show. It appears creator and creation must work together in an attitude of cooperation for excellence to be recognized, realized, and received.

Keeping in mind that this passage follows the chiastic poem concerning the specifics of designated time as Qoheleth sees it played out under the sun, the plain sense of "made everything suitable" is that there is beauty in the gift of life, when life is discovered as moments contained within the life of God. Here *'olam* ("time") is not so concerned with the scope of time—i.e., "eternity," not "past and future" (NRSV)—as that which transcends human understandings of time. It seems to suggest the mystery of time, thus transcendence. And, weaving the thread of reimagined wisdom thought that is grounded in the Genesis tradition, Qoheleth notes that God has appointed a special quality for humanity: the ability to commune with transcendence which is in the fabric of their inner being. Yet, this quality is still held within the parameters of gift, not an ability generated outside or apart from the creator-God. Ultimately, time as humanity can grasp it—beginnings and endings—does not contain God's activity. God's activity, rather, stretches far beyond what humanity can perceive. It is a transcendence that mysteriously shows up as immanent.

This leads Qoheleth to a realization: that there is "nothing better" for humanity. Here is found the *tob*, which is the "good" or "good things." Often translated as a negative clause, it is set as a comparative with no direct object, thus "the best thing." Now the specific cooperation from a few sentences back is addressed: "receive happiness." This is the best thing that humanity can do in life, because it is God's gift. In this simple statement of epiphany, Qoheleth suggests that God freely gives to all. Thus, those who are eating and drinking and discovering goodness "amid all their toil" are those who "receive." This defies the notions of God's immutability that have been imposed on the Ecclesiastes text. God is freely giving a gift that can be rejected, not determining willy-nilly who will be happy and who will not. The excellence is given to, and available for, all!

This line of thought continues, addressing God's actions specifically. The *hayah*, translated as "endures" (NRSV), does not necessarily mean an act or action performed once and finished from then on. Nor would this notion hold with the Hebraic concept of creation that understands God as continually in the process of creating. Qoheleth concludes that God is continuing to act; God's activity in the earth will continue. Qoheleth, very much in line with the Christian humanist trajectory, will only accept newness as part of a continuum. To deny or reject the past is to relinquish the fullness of the present and to prevent any desirable future. The activity of God gives us a paradigm for intended human activity. God's activity is simply *what is* (it exists) and "there is nothing to add nor subtract." This is nothing more than a qualitative statement on the *hayah* of God's activity in and with creation. The qualitative statement is difficult to render in English, so I added "they are complete." This is connected to the theme of transcendence that Qoheleth has realized. Such discovery and realization leads him to the conclusion that God's ongoing creating activity is beautiful and right and complete, however much beyond humanity's understanding it may be. Yet there is purpose to God's activity; a call that is seeking response from all humanity: "worship." To "stand in awe before him" (NRSV) is the Hebraic understanding and posture of worship. And this is not simply a spiritual state, nor an attitudinal adjustment of the heart. Rather, it suggests a holistic involvement of the whole body, an action. It is an active response of worship as life lived in reception of the gift of excellence. Worship that has the old as its foundation and situates the old through re-narration constitutes the newness. Qoheleth is foreshadowing what the Catholic philosopher Josef Pieper called the "everlasting festival."

As a final statement on this whole section dealing with time, Qoheleth poetically sums up all time as dramatically, mysteriously, and profoundly being wrapped in the life of God. The point is not the placement of time, but the placement of humanity's relation to God within time as revealed in the life of God. Newness emerges from the interplay of the divine-human relationship. God is seeking something from humanity. In fact, God is seeking by sending out a call, an invitation to respond. It is the "response" of verse 10. Qoheleth realizes that humanity is invited by God to pursue what seems to be a hidden newness. And this hidden thing is the something beyond the nothing—the *hebel*. It is only discovered in response to God's gracious gift, by cooperating with God's creating actions. Those who would receive the gift of excellence, who would discover the newness, have their eyes open to the beauty of the gift of life.

And with eyes wide open, they can pursue what is hidden.

Interlude

God the Community

WHAT IS GOD LIKE?

Sometimes I imagine God as a Community.

Each individual contributes to the whole. God the Community is not fully God without each member. The universal cannot be itself without every single particular.

There is the strange iconoclastic teacher, Qoheleth. He questions and he questions and he questions.

There is Virginia, who is perhaps wiser than all of us, patiently listening to the melancholy Albert, who may just want to sink the boat.

There is the skeptical Friedrich sharing a laugh and playing cards with the orthodox Gilbert.

There is Soren and all his constituent selves, who cannot stand the religious institution, investigating some stars with his new friend Erasmus, who will always be Catholic.

There is Therese, who never wanted to be a saint, watching an ancient Weaver at her craft, while a Little Boy makes a delightful mess of the fabric scraps strewn across the floor.

There is Randy the professor, more alive than we dared to hope.

There is Michel with his essays, Socrates with his questions, Vives with his humanity.

There are the millions through human history; the destitute, and even some aristocrats; all the powerless, minorities, outsiders, liminal dwellers, and even some majority stakeholders, some powerful.

And there is you.

And there is me.

And we value each other because we know what it is like to be an *other*. And we know what it is like to be nothing. And we know what it is like to be something.

God the Community changes continually while maintaining a steady core that is more ancient than time: this core is a love. Love like a dance of the first community of three that flows over into all the rest of everything.

And this is God.

8

Gift, Reception, Return

I see that it is enough to realize one's nothingness, and give ourself wholly, like a child, into the arms of the good God. Leaving to great souls, great minds, the fine books I can't understand, I rejoice to be little.

—ST. THERESE OF LISIEUX

THIS BRILLIANTLY HONEST AND blazingly innovative new breed of sapiential poet, Qoheleth, comes near the end of life and discovers that excellence of life is gifted to all humanity by the God who is continually moving from creation to new creation. The nothing is not the last word. Qoheleth looks beyond the nothing of life lived outside the life of God and perceives the excellent something that is made available by God's gracious gift. If I were to ever construct a full-fledged commentary on Ecclesiastes, I'd suggest a thematic framework that persists as gift, reception, and return.

Qoheleth instructs the hearer to "Send out your bread upon the waters, for after many days it will return to you" (11:1). We've been given a gift ("bread"), we can choose to receive it, and then, when the time is right, return our bread out on the waters. The whole book of Ecclesiastes is a book about the process, the journey of discovery; and here lies an amazing one. As he so often does, Qoheleth is reimagining familiar usages. Thus, "bread" carries the suggestion of anything one receives as a gift. So, could it be that Qoheleth is calling for the hearer to give away even the very life that has been gifted? And if so, could this gifted life, once given away, be found again? Our prophet-teacher-philosopher-poet is here coloring outside the lines, again, which he does so well. The sounds of the creator-God, who became wisdom in the flesh in the identity of Jesus Christ, must certainly ring in our ears: "For those who want to save their life will lose it, and those who lose their life for my sake will save it" (Luke 9:24). That's so foolish.

And yet, perhaps, those who have received the gift—not those that have just been given the gift, for that's all of us, but those who have actually opened the gift in an action of reception, who have discovered the beauty of life as contained within the life of God, and are living lives of actionable worship that foreshadow an everlasting festival—must not cling to the gift, but are invited to cast it away. This return to God of the gift given is a great paradox. Yet, it was the wisdom incarnated among us in Christ. And that life is the life extended to humanity in the present and even, as Qoheleth would say, under the sun. Yes, excellence can be received now, and lived as a life of reception and return in cooperation with the God who freely gives.

We must now revisit the *hebel*: the nothingness, the vapor, the wind, the uselessness. From his side of all that is useless, does Qoheleth see anything that lasts? From his side of nothingness, does he dare to hope there is something beyond it? And if so, what is that something? Though schooled in the wisdom tradition, Qoheleth is wise enough to know that our language will always be, in some measure, inadequate to bear the reason that we name. And yet he knows we must attempt to bear it. This is, after all, the gift given us; it is life. Qoheleth is hinting at the something on the other side of the nothing. Qoheleth's language is consistently apophatic—a fancy word which has to do with negating what we think we know. He sees that God is not as God has been traditionally assumed in the sapiential view, nor the synchronic understanding of Deuteronomic thought. The particulars of what we know, or what we think we know, cannot be all there is to reality. Qoheleth is not deceived by nominalism. And yet, we have a limited grammar with which to try to talk about God. One of my former theology professors called this a meontic conundrum. "Meontic" is a word that comes from a Greek root meaning "that which is not." So when we try to describe the attributes of divinity that have not been witnessed nor given grammar in our reality, we are essentially attempting the impossible.

John Keats, the early-nineteenth-century romantic poet, once illustrated this notion when he said of his fellow poet, Lord Byron: "There is this great difference between us. He describes what he sees; I describe what I imagine." That's a fine way to understand our meontic attempt to discuss God. We are at the same time trying to describe some of what we've seen and a lot of what we imagine.

If the God we don't yet know is this something on the other side of all that is under the sun, then must this God be named? What I mean to say is, could this God ever be packaged in humanity's boxes? It seems that the gift of life, given by this God who gives, cannot be contained. That's how nothing becomes something. Streaks of gray across a dusk-illumined sky. They pursue each other. They fade. We pursue their fading. We rejoice in our littleness. And then, somehow, nothing becomes something by the grace of God.

So, let me receive my bread. Let me receive my life. Let me do so while recognizing my own nothingness, my own inability to gain excellence. Let me embrace God's gift of excellent life, receiving it as I would any gift I really, truly wanted. For if I take the metaphorical package, wrapped in fine paper and gilded with a bow, set it to one side, perhaps even place it in my backpack so it can go with me wherever I go, but I never open up the gift, have I actually ever received it? No. I must open it. And in so doing, I open a life of hard work, but a life that has potential for excellence and gain, a life that can be a long and enduring exercise of active worship. A life where worship is the lifestyle, because I return that received gift.

Then let me throw my bread out on the waters. Let it get soggy, and ruined, and drowned in the mysterious waters swirling with molecules of transcendence and atoms of immanence. Let me send out that excellent life until it is exhausted, until it has been spent, until it has become something it could not become any other way. Let the gain of this act be experienced through its loss. Let the paradox go recognized but unanswered. Let the newness of something ancient and old and mysterious engulf me like those waters that drench my bread.

Finally, let the bread return to me. Let it return only because I first let it go. Let that stand as something I cannot begin to explain. Let the purpose of this wisdom be in the actively contemplated living of it, not in its perfect completion. Let my littleness be as it is, and let me be dependent on something beyond all the nothing I can't explain.

Let me, let Qoheleth, let us all raise a glass as we participate in the beginnings of the everlasting festival, made more human by the doing of such a thing, made more excellent by a strange gift, made more common in the true spirit of community.

Postlude

The Elephant in the Room, or
The God We Don't Yet Know

I HAVE A NAME for God: Jesus of Nazareth. Maybe you have a different name. Maybe you struggle to grant a divine being any real or possible existence. I think of this God, at turns, as a weaver, as a young child, as a community, and so much more.

But I don't know.

Neither do you.

And that's fine. Because this is the elephant in the room of faith, in the room of knowledge, in the room of reason. It is a beast that roams these arenas effortlessly. But it's fine, because we can name it. So, let's do so:

We don't know all we think we know about God.

There.

Done.

The bravest of us have been willing to admit this for centuries. Like Socrates, for example. In Plato's dramatization of Socrates' defense of himself when he was put on trial for corrupting the young—which is a dishonest way to suggest he was inviting the young to think for themselves—Socrates insisted he couldn't corrupt others if he himself knew nothing at all. But then again, maybe that is the profoundest wisdom of all: to admit that one knows nothing. Socrates told the court of a time years before when he was called before the Oracle at Delphi and was told by the god that he was wise. Did Socrates accept this word from the divine as truth? No. He questioned such a declaration. He spent years investigating and studying all manner of humanity to see who was wise. He tells the court that he met many who thought themselves wise, many who others thought wise, and yet all these supposedly wise people actually knew very little. Eventually, Socrates admits that maybe in his ability to admit he knows nothing, he may just be wise. For many who are ostensibly wise do not humbly entertain the notion that they may not know all they think they know, nor what all others say of them that they know. But even this conclusion about the divine oracle was a tentative conclusion. Socrates was wise enough to know that he may be proven wrong. Indeed, had he been proven wrong he might have lived a bit longer. Instead, he was found guilty of affording others the opportunity to think, and he was condemned to die. All this proved the oracle right, after all.

Some have suggested that Plato's Socrates is to be read ironically, in the sense that Socrates' humility is false. Instead of questioning incessantly because he really doesn't know the answers, he makes fools of all his conversation partners, because he already knows he knows more than them. I find this unsatisfying and a cowardly reading of the texts. Yes, Socrates should be read ironically. But this irony is a humble dissembling; it is saying less than one thinks. And the opposite of this irony is boastfulness. May we all be a little more ironic, like Socrates.

And Qoheleth, too. Why did he pose so many questions, many of them repeated over and over again? Maybe it is because he truly did not know. Or at least he was willing to be humbly ironic in expressing less than he thought. Did he ignore the God who could not be equated to what the wisest of his age and before him had declared God to be? Or did he rather know that he did not know this God well enough to make such grand and concrete declarations? If so, may we all be a little more humble, like Qoheleth.

If the greatest, and bravest, and most humane struggle of our human existence is to contemplate and experience what is good and beautiful and true, how can we possibly know what those things are? Jesus of Nazareth, the individual that millions throughout history have deemed to be divine—and not just divine, but the God of Hebrew Scripture in the flesh—was once called good. Surely, we can call him good, can we not, regardless of our persuasion on the issue of divinity? Surely, we can write some songs about the goodness of this Jesus, yes? And we have. But his response to being called good was essentially, "No one is good, not even me." Socrates was called wise, and he responded by creating questions around that declaration. Jesus was called good, and he responded in kind by creating questions around the notion.

There are none who are good. And yet we want to pursue, and experience, and contemplate the good. There are none wise enough to declaim what is true. And yet we want to know what is true. How can we reconcile such paradoxes?

Maybe the answer is not an answer, but a question. A question we can live in. A multitude of questions, a sea of questions. Questions encompassing all the stuff we don't really know, and don't yet know. And that's a lot.

In addition to the elephant in the room, which may not be an elephant after all—we don't yet know all we think we know about God—there other wrinkles in the fabric of our assumed knowledge. For example, we think we know why a rock falls from a cliff to the ground below. Thanks to the work of Isaac Newton, we know this is because of an unassailable scientific law. It's more than a theory, because it can be proven over and over again. And it cannot yet be disproven. That rock falls because it must be subject to the laws of the universe. These are laws we have scribbled out over the history of our growing knowledge. No inanimate and lifeless object like a rock could dare call such a law into question. Yet, roughly two millennia before falling apples led Newton to the potential iron-clad case for all falling things, Aristotle said a rock would fall to earth because it desires to descend. "How silly," we might say. How primitive, and misguided, and uninformed. And yet, if we allow ourselves to sit with some questions, we might find such a notion is not as preposterous as we in our modern wisdom first assumed. Which is a truer statement of the falling rock? Which is more right? How do we know which to choose? And which more authentically describes what is? Could there be something like a rock's desire beyond the nothing established by universal laws?

Or consider dark matter. It is not there, and yet it is. Our theories and our mathematics suggest there has to be more of it than the matter we can see and discern. We don't really know dark matter, yet we have faith that it is there. Why? Does its absence make it more real? Can we measure nothingness? Could there be something not yet discernible holding together all we can currently measure? And how would we know? How could we know?

I wonder if we have all our answers too much at the ready. I wonder if we look at the world through a Google lens that insists there will always be an answer to every question. If so, I wonder if a Qoheleth lens is a more authentic way to live with *what is* about ourselves, our world, and all we may not yet know.

I wonder if we have lost humble irony.

In the process of raising three children, my wife and I have been through years of kid questions. Any parent worth their stuff knows what I'm talking about.

Take an age-old question like, "Daddy, why is the sky blue?"

No matter what answer I give, the next question will be, "Why?"

And no matter how many times I answer, there is always a potential next "why."

With my oldest child, I got good at giving easy answers that would shortcircuit the endless litany of whys. I regret that. It took a few rounds with all our kids, but I eventually began to resist the temptation to provide easy answers. Instead, I began leaning into something bigger and braver. It took a bit of humbling on my part—my lifelong story, in fact, is one of humbling; but that's for another book. I now am willing to respond to my kids' questions with an honest, "I don't know." And, when I do this, a whole universe of possibilities open up to exploration. I can become a partner with my child in investigating the questions, searching for meaning, learning how to learn, and living with uncertainty. Maybe this little slice of my life has become something that is good, and beautiful, and true.

Throughout this book, we've considered three of Qoheleth's questions in various ways. Have I answered his questions? I doubt it, since that hasn't been the intent of this project. His questions may not have answers we can realize. But there are a variety of responses—not answers—to the questions which we can embrace. All these centuries after Qoheleth first posed the questions, they are still pertinent for us. What is the point of all our work? Is there ever anything new? What is the purpose of wisdom?

And we have our own unanswered questions, too, don't we?

- What is good?
- What is beautiful?
- What is true?
- Is God real?
- What is God like?
- What am I like?
- How do we best love others?
- Where is meaning in life found?

There are lots of individuals, organizations, institutions, and traditions that offer answers to these questions. There are also a dizzying amount of books that offer to provide concrete answers. I admire Qoheleth for admitting he doesn't know the answers, but being willing to flesh out some possible responses to the questions. The primary response he offers is, of course, to never stop wrestling with the questions. This book has attempted to be something like that. And yet, "something like" is never the actual thing. Another personality in the Hebrew Scripture, Ezekiel, talked about seeing "something like" the presence of God. It was God, but his words failed in describing the divine. His words could not fully communicate what he didn't yet know. He could only convey "something like." And maybe that's the whole point.

We think we know lots of things: about ourselves, the universe, divine things. I'm not so sure. And maybe I'm wrong. And that's just fine. But if you will allow me to once again, I'll leave you with a few more questions.

- What if we were brave and humble enough to acknowledge, publicly and repeatedly, that we don't know even what we think we do know?

- What if we held our understanding of divine things and of ourselves in the tension of questions with a soft touch, able to let go when our understanding changes?

- What if the things we name "nothing" and the things we name "something" aren't diametrically opposed, but are more closely related to each other than we ever dared to imagine?

I don't know the answers. But I'm sure enough—or crazy enough—to suggest that in our individual and shared responses to these questions, in our undaunted willingness to live with these questions, we might see, we might experience, we might catch a glimpse of something like the God we don't yet know.

Bibliography

Brown, William P. *Character in Crisis: A Fresh Approach to the Wisdom Literature of the Old Testament.* Grand Rapids: Eerdmans, 1996.

Bruni, Leonardo. "On the Study of Literature." In *The Great Tradition: Classic Readings on What It Means to Be an Educated Human Being,* edited by Richard M. Gamble, 333–41. Wilmington, NC: ISI, 2009.

Camus, Albert. *The Rebel: An Essay on Man in Revolt.* Translated by Anthony Bower. New York: Vintage, 2008.

Chesterton, G. K. "The New Jerusalem." In *The Collected Works of G. K. Chesterton,* edited by James V. Schall, 191–422. Vol. 20. San Francisco: Ignatius, 2001.

Delitzsch, Franz. *Proverbs, Ecclesiastes, Song of Solomon.* Vol. 6 of *Commentary on the Old Testament in Ten Volumes,* edited by C. F. Keil and F. Delitzsch, translated by M. G. Easton. Grand Rapids: Eerdmans, 1989.

Erasmus, Desiderius. "The Antibarbarians." In *The Erasmus Reader,* translated by Erika Rummel, 31–43. Toronto: University of Toronto Press, 2003.

Kierkegaard, Søren. *Either/Or: A Fragment of Life.* Edited by Victor Eremita. Translated by Alastair Hannay. London: Penguin, 1992.

Murphy, Roland. *The Tree of Life: An Exploration of Biblical Wisdom Literature.* 3rd ed. Grand Rapids: Eerdmans, 2002.

Newman, John Henry. *The Idea of a University.* Edited by Frank M. Turner. New Haven: Yale University Press, 1996.

Nietzsche, Friedrich. *Will to Power.* Translated by Walter Kaufmann. New York: Random House, 1967.

Pieper, Josef. *Leisure: The Basis of Culture.* San Francisco: Ignatius, 2009.

Vico, Giambattista. "On the Proper Order of Studies." In *On Humanistic Education: Six Inaugural Orations, 1699-1707,* translated by Gian Galeazzo Visconti, 123–40. Ithaca, NY: Cornell University Press, 1993.

Victore, Hugo De Sancto. *The Didascalicon of Hugh of St. Victor: A Medieval Guide to the Arts.* Translated by Jerome Taylor. New York: Columbia University Press, 1991.

26056164R00057

Made in the USA
Columbia, SC
05 September 2018